a collection of Short Screenplays

Peter John Ross

Columbus, Ohio, USA

ISBN 9798648242142
LCCN

Printed in the United States of Awesome.

Preface

In early days of cinema, there was nothing but the short form. As cinema grew over the decades and feature length flourished, the short subject did not falter. Saturday matinees were filled with 3 minute to 20 minute short subject live action films, like the Little Rascals, Laurel and Hardy, Flash Gordon, and other serials. By the end of the 1960's the short subject was relegated to specialized film festivals.

In the new millennia, the short subject has made a drastic return due to digital video and the Internet. Filmmaking has become affordable and with it, scripting in the short form has increased. Presented here are several short film screenplays for use as public domain pieces, either for practice or any professional usage.

I offer unto the public these screenplays to be made or remade in any fashion the filmmaker requires with no other cost than the price of this printed publication. Consider that the "royalty" cost to use my work. All I ask is that I receive an onscreen credit for either "written by Peter John Ross" or "Based on a Screenplay by Peter John Ross".

If you should endeavor to make one of these into a motion

picture, then by all means know that these are open to interpretation, editorial choices, and exist at the whim of the directors, producers, and anyone that affects a movie from the page to the screen, even a tiny 320x240 screen on YouTube or a 75 foot long movie screen.

Don't feel obligated to follow the scripts exactly. Make your own choices. I know that when I made some of these, I didn't stay married to the script, as it was solely a blue print and most people learn that the ideas on paper rarely translate perfectly to the real world, so make these your own.

-   Peter John Ross

Acknowledgements

I gratefully acknowledge the wonderful actors, producers, and various craftspeople I've worked with for the past 20 years, ever teaching me new things about filmmaking.

In particular, I want to thank the siblings Joanne and John Fromes. They have stuck by me for over a decade, even after I cheated with John's wife and caused a divorce and made the holidays exceptionally awkward for them. John has continued to be a collaborator, even when I showed blatant favoratism towards his sister Joanne.

Joanne also stood by after I had a rather cruel daliance with her girlfriend as well and took her to Mexico. Still, Joanne create amazing art for me since. These people are the backbone of my career.

Contents

COLLECTION OF SHORT SCREENPLAYS

BACK OFFICE

This is actuall 6 screenplays combined, each one from a different genre, and meant to be demonstrating some kind of versatility as a writer and director. The intent was to avoid being pigeon-holed into a single genre like poor Wes Craven who can only do Horror films because that is what he did successfully first. If Wes Craven were to attempt to make a romantic comedy, he would be getting in line with producers the same as any first time director because he isn't a proven commodity for that type of movie.

To try to avoid that "Wes Craven Syndrome", I wanted to tackle several genres at once, as a writer and director. I will notate some per each segment.

Long before there was even the British original version of THE OFFICE, I wanted to tackle the idea of a multi-facted look at office culture. There was mostly humor, but also some realities. Granted, it was a stretch to work in the action-chase story, but I did. Within these screenplays are loose links to tie all six stories together, following a voice mail as it gets passed from one story to another. This was so I could economically use all 6 shorts together as one movie to save money on film festival submissions, or I could edit that dialogue out and send them off individually.

THE MANHATTAN PROJECT

This is a particurlaly and intentionally gross movie and subject matter. I believed very much in the ability to tap into the basic concept that everyone deals with bathroom etiquette issues often, especially in an office environment. This one was based on a very real person and sadly, very real incidents when I was working as a broker at a large bank.

EXT. OFFICE BUILDING - MORNING

It's 8:00 A.M. and there are already several cars parked outside the building with an indiscriminate corporation housed inside. Like all the buildings in this corporate park, there is no logo on the front, just the address numbers.

INT. OFFICE HALL, IN FRONT OF MEN'S ROOM

JIM BLACK, gets a drink at the fountain. He wipes his lips, then enters the Men's Room.

INT. MEN'S ROOM

Jim casually walks over to the urinal, looks down then, unzips his pants and lets fly the urination. As he is going, the door opens behind him and enters PHIL, or as he is known "BIG PHIL", a man who easily weighs 320 plus.

Phil is already unbuckling his pants and doing some kind of emergency dance as he waddles to a stall.

Once the door to the stall closes, Big Phil exhales loudly.

BACK OFFICE

PHIL
(with resignation)
Oh boy, here it comes.

CU of Jim's face as the flatulence noises begin. He winces, then the first wave of odors hits and Jim can hardly stand up. He hits the wall next to him and grabs his nose.

From within the stall comes the sound of rustling. Jim turns his head slowly in the direction of the stall. Chomping noises & the distinct crunching of chips can be heard.

PHIL
Goodness gracious! Another one.

Another wave of flatulence and the odor hit Jim like a brick. He scrambles from the men's room, just as the bag of chips hits the floor.

INT. OFFICE HALL, IN FRONT OF MEN'S ROOM

Jim is covered in sweat and his face is lined. He resembles a Vietnam vet or a hostage just released.

EDWARD walks up and sees Jim put his head in his hands.

EDWARD
Jim, are you okay? Jim, what happened
to you?

JIM
(frantic and stuttering)

Oh my God...I was in the men's room...
and Phil came in... and he.. and he...

                    EDWARD
Oh my God, you were in there
          (points to the men's room)
during 'the Manhattan Project'?

                    JIM
Is Phil always like that?

                    EDWARD
Hey, there's a reason I walk up to the
gas station on the corner just to take
a piss.

Phil exits the men's room.

                    PHIL
Excuse me, there boys.

As Phil passes on his way down the hall, a bit of the
smell follows through. Both Edward and Jim wince.

                    EDWARD
Let's get out of here.

                    JIM
Jesus, there's two doors and you can
still smell it out here.

They leave.

INT. EDWARDS CUBE

Edward sits at his desk and types a message and Jim sits

BACK OFFICE

at a chair in the cube.

EDWARD

So there I was one day, just got back
from lunch and I really had to go.

INT. MEN'S ROOM - FLASHBACK
Edward is sitting there, reading a paper.

EDWARD (V.O.)

I was just getting to the sports
section when I hear the sound of Phil
enter in.

Edward's POV of the feet of Phil walking from one stall
to the next. The door to Edwards stall gets tugged and
pulled. Phil's eyes try to peek through the slits
between the door and the frame.

CU of Edward's eyes going wide as they meet the eyes of
Phil peeking through the slits.

INT. EDWARDS CUBE

Edward finishes typing something on the PC.

EDWARD

I mean, is it just me, or is that so
wrong? If the door is locked, you
don't need to know who's inside. That's
just not right.

JIM

What about the updates?

5

                    EDWARD
Updates?

                    JIM
Yeah, the constant descriptions or
sudden proclamations about what is
happening.

                                    CUT TO:

INT. MEN'S ROOM - FLASHBACK

All we can see are Phil's feet inside a stall.

                    PHIL
Oh boy, get ready.

From another angle.

                    PHIL
Ahhhhhhhh. That's more like it.

From the side angle.

                    PHIL
Just a little bit more.

Seeing the candy wrappers hit the floor and the
crunching noises.

                                    CUT TO:

INT. EDWARDS CUBE

Edward stares, his mouth agape.

BACK OFFICE

                        EDWARD
            And what about the eating?

                         JIM
            To me, that's worse than the
            commentary. I don't think you should be
            putting in, while you sending out.
            Dude, ever wonder why you're overweight
            ? His idea of a snack is bigger than a
            four course meal to me.

                        EDWARD
            I remember the last straw to me, it was
            free pizza Friday ...

                                        CUT TO:

INT. MEN'S ROOM - FLASHBACK

Edward is washing his hands, shown from the mirror POV,
and Phil enters, doing his "Pee Pee Dance" struggling
with his belt even as he enters the room.

                         PHIL
                (as he waddles over)
            That Pizza goes right through me...

The door to the stall closes and the flatulence noises
begin, mixed with a sound that can best be described as
a bushel of apples being poured into a pale of water.

                                        CUT TO:

INT. EDWARDS CUBE

Edward moves the mouse on his computer.

EDWARD
What I heard then was like a bushel of
apples being poured into a small pale
of water.

JIM
I'm never going to use the men's room
here again, now.

EDWARD
I've got something that might help us.

Edward walks out of his cube, then returns a moment
later with a printout in his hands.

EDWARD
(hands the sheet to Jim)
Here, read this, I have to check my
voice mail.

JIM
"The bathroom rules of etiquette..."

Edward presses the number on his phone to access his
voice mail. He listens while noodling with his pen on a
legal pad.

VOICE MAIL (V.O.)
Hey, this is Noel. I was just in this
meeting and we were discussing the
merger. I swear if those guys from
Cincinnati don't pull their heads out
of the ground, we'll never get
everything in line in time for the
conversion. Do you remember how I told

you that Roger Downs went to Vegas with
us last time? Well, he was getting so
drunk that he couldn't stand up. It's
amazing to me to see a guy like that
heaving in a toilet like a college
freshman...

                    EDWARD
                   (to Jim)
There's a wierd voicemail here from
Noel Wilson, but I don't think it's for
me.

              VOICE MAIL (CON'T)
I know you met Roger at the National
Training last year, so I thought you'd
get a kick out of that. Anyway, I was
just coming out of the meeting and I
was thinking, God, I loved giving it to
you from behind...

Edward's pen flies out of his hand, and his eyes go very
wide.

              VOICE MAIL (CON'T)
You were so good. I loved being inside
of you. I can't wait until next week
when I get to come back to town and we
can get together again. You did things
to me that I've never had done.

                                        CUT TO:

INT. MEN'S ROOM

Phil enters, does his "Pee Pee Dance"/waddle and sees on
the mirror, and the stall doors, inside and out are

printouts of the "Bathroom etiquette" as well as a pre schoolers "How To potty train" brochure.

They are taped everywhere and fresh cans of potpourri.

CONSPIRACY THEORIES

Being of the "Tarantino" Generation of filmmaking, I lovede pop culture and loved the use of pop culture references in dialogue. Being also somewhat of a technical geek, I knew the IT guys very well. Many of them view Bill Gates and Microsoft as an "evil empire" and get quite conspiratorial in their beliefs. This was my poking a little fun at that, as well as Star Trek.

INT. COMPUTER TECHNOLOGIES AREA - DAY

This is a group of five cubes in the back of the building where computers lay wide open, wires dangling and everything is a mess and the eccentric people who work here have their own order to the universe.

Sitting at his desk, MARK CATON, early 20's has a screwdriver in one hand and is tinkering with a motherboard as the phone rings.

                    MARK CATON
                (hits the speaker phone)
            Technologies, this is Mark.

                    DANIEL (V.O.)
                (from speaker phone)
            Hi Mark, this Daniel Lewis, and I'm
            having some trouble with my computer.

BACK OFFICE

MARK CATON
Have you filled out the survey?

DANIEL (V.O.)
What survey?

MARK CATON
All new problems have to go through the
forms before I can help you, so open up
the envelope marked "Technologies
Support", do you have that?

DANIEL (V.O.)
Yes, it's here.
    (tearing noises over the
    speaker phone)
Got it.

MARK CATON
Now let's go through this together.

DANIEL
"Question number one : describe the
problem", okay my problem is that I
turned the computer on and nothing
happened.

MARK CATON
Question number two...

DANIEL
"Describe the problem accurately.",
okay I turned the power on and nothing
is still happening.

MARK CATON
Uh huh.

DANIEL
"Number three : Speculate wildly about
the cause" , well that's funny because
I was gonna say that I think it has
something to do with how the word
processor and our email work together.

MARK CATON
Yeah, that's likely. Let's keep moving
on.

DANIEL
"Number four : Problem severity A.
Minor, B. Minor, C. Minor, D. Trivial",
well seeing that I can't see anything
at all, I'd say it's severe.

MARK CATON
You must have done well on your
S.A.T.'s with the multiple choice. I
can see this is going to take some
time, so let me help you get through
the rest of this.
     (puts the screw driver down &
     picks up a piece of paper)
Have you tried to fix it yourself?

DANIEL
Yes.

MARK CATON
Did you make it worse?

BACK OFFICE

DANIEL
No, it's the same.

MARK CATON
Have you had a friend who "knows all
about computers" try to fix the
computer for you?

DANIEL
No.

MARK CATON
Have you read the manual?

DANIEL
Yes.

MARK CATON
Are you absolutely certain you read the
manual?

DANIEL
Yes.

MARK CATON
If you read the manual, do you think
you understood it?

DANIEL
Yes.

MARK CATON
If "yes", then explain why you can;'t
fix this yourself.

DANIEL
It didn't cover this particular error.

MARK CATON
Are you sure you aren't imagining the
problem?

DANIEL
Does it actually say that in the
questionnaire?

MARK CATON
It's question number twelve, sir. Does
the clock on your VCR blink twelve
O'clock?

DANIEL
No.

MARK CATON
Do you have any independant witnesses
to your computer problem?

DANIEL
No.

MARK CATON
Is there anyone else you could blame
the problem on?

DANIEL
I guess not.

MARK CATON
Well, then let try a little cause and
effect. You say there's no picture on

your screen. Does the little light come
on when you turn the power on the
monitor?

              DANIEL
No.

           MARK CATON
Have you looked under the computer to
see if the moniter is plugged into the
wall?

              DANIEL
    (long pause)
Shit! I'm an idiot.

           MARK CATON
Thank you for calling technologies.
    (hits the speakerphone
    button)
Retard.

Enter JOHN PATTERSON, the youngest of the Tech crew, and
also HUGH SIMON, a much older techie guy enter the cubicle
area.

              HUGH
    (to John)
And that's why they do that when you
put the dollar bill in your mouth and
you lie on the table.
    (to Mark)
Anything going on here?

MARK CATON
Just another user not knowing that you
have to plug in a moniter to get it to
turn on.

HUGH
I think the average human should not be
allowed to touch a computer.

JOHN
Did you see the new Gateway and the
IEEE 1394 ports are now a part of the
package.

MARK CATON
They suck.

HUGH
I'm still using the four pin port and I
think it's good.

JOHN
Yeah, but the IE1394's are so much
better.

HUGH
Not that much better.

JOHN
You're just stuck with your ancient
1999 model computer which belongs in a
museum next to the crossbow.

Enter EDWARD, from earlier.

BACK OFFICE

EDWARD

Hey fellahs.

HUGH

Mister Man. How's it going?

EDWARD

Not bad, not bad. Did you know the server for all of the accounting department just went down?

HUGH

God damn it! I just checked on that.

Hugh and John both exit. Edward leans into Hugh's cube.

EDWARD

Is Elizabeth from the consulting firm going back today?

HUGH

Yes. Her flight leaves at 10:30 A.M.

EDWARD

Dave and Rick are flying in at 10:36, do you mind picking them up?

HUGH

No, not at all.

EDWARD

(whispering)

You know that one girl, the real hot one who always wears the three size too small skirts and four size too small sweaters?

                    HUGH
That would be Miss Christy LaHood.
                    EDWARD
That's the one. Well, I forwarded you a
little voice mail that was left for
her. I think you'll like it.

Edward leaves. Hugh picks up his phone and presses in
his ID number.

                    VOICE MAIL
... I know you met Roger at the
National Training last year, so I
thought you'd get a kick out of that.
Anyway, I was just coming out of the
meeting and I was thinking, God, I
loved giving it to you from behind...

Hugh starts laughing.

INT. SERVER ROOM - DAY

John is handing a small screwdriver to Mark, who is
        halfway under a worktable, covered in wires and
cables.

                    MARK CATON
..So I think it's perfectly obvious.

                    JOHN
You think Star Trek is communist
propaganda?

                    MARK CATON
Think about it. There's no money in the

BACK OFFICE

24th century, everyone works for the
government, and there's no religion. If
that's not an exact representation of
communism, I don't know what is. It's
all very Marxist.

                    JOHN
               (bored)
          That's interesting.

Hugh enters.

                    HUGH
          What was it?

                    MARK CATON
          God damn Microsoft.

                    HUGH
          It was that last service pack, wasn't
          it?

                    JOHN
          Microsoft would not release a service
          pack that wasn't beta tested.

                    MARK CATON
               (to John)
          You do realize that Bill Gates
          expressly sends out versions of Windows
          with flaws so that we have to buy the
          upgrades.

                    JOHN
          Oh, come on.

MARK CATON
It's true. It's the ultimate money
making scheme.

HUGH
Release a product you know to be
flawed, then force the public to pay
more money to buy a working version.

MARK CATON
I read about it on a news group on the
internet. They said there are
disgruntled Microsoft employees who
smuggled documents out about how Bill
Gates bribes U.S. senators and that he
has a back door bug, so that anyone on
the internet can get hit by Microsoft's
secret scanning program.

HUGH
Anyone surfing the web can have their
whole computer scanned by Microsoft's
programmers and if the bots find any
unlicensed software, they'll delete
your whole computer.

JOHN
Stop it you guys. That's total B.S.
That's illegal.

HUGH
You know that legal junk you just click
"yes" to every time you load a
program?

JOHN
Yeah?

MARK CATON
When you clicked on "yes", you forego
any and all rights. You should read
that license agreement sometime. It's
like a unibomber manifesto.

JOHN
Did it ever occur to you guys that
maybe there are maybe fifteen to
seventeen thousand programmers, all of
which are human and make mistakes,
working on the same complex operating
system, don't you think it's possible,
that a few mistakes would get by?

MARK CATON
You are so naive.

JOHN
Arghhh!

HUGH
I need a volunteer.

MARK CATON
For what?

HUGH
I need someone to drop off that
consultant from Chicago at the airport
and also pick up two execs from
accounts receivable.

MARK CATON
Which consultant?

HUGH
Elizabeth.

JOHN
I'll do it. I'll go.

HUGH
Okay, just make sure you're back after
lunch. We have to reset the UNIX box.

JOHN
(as he hands the tools to
Hugh)
No problemo, chief.

John leaves.

ASPYXIATED HEART

In the original screenplay idea, the character of JOHN from the previous story, CONSPIRACY THEORIES, would go from that story into this one, but the actor was not as experienced as I preferred, so I just made a new character for ASPHYXIATED HEART. This story represents a "chick flick", or love story that appeals mostly to females.

EXT. AIRPORT - DAY

Establishing shot of an airport, somewhere in the U.S.
Taxi cabs, shuttles and cars are all over the place,
trying to get in and out of the bustle of the city.

INT. GATE 37B - NIGHT

Boarding has not begun yet. Everyone looks like their in
a state of intense malaise. There is the old sloppy
business man with his copy of USA today, and the old
couples in their matching pants and shirts.

Sitting near the window and with the actual gate behind
them are JOHN PATTERSON, 28 and blonde with short
cropped hair, and ELIZABETH DAVIS, 24 year old brunette
with long flowing hair. She has the bags near here feet
and she stares at the ceiling. She chews on gum slowly.
John stares at the floor, swishing his feet back and
forth.

                         JOHN
             So the flight's delayed.

                       ELIZABETH
                     (long beat)
             I guess so.

     Another long pause.

                         JOHN
             I once waited in an airport for seven
             hours waiting for a flight.

                       ELIZABETH
             Where were you going?

                         JOHN
             Philadelphia.

                    ELIZABETH
Nice museums there.

                    JOHN
Yeah....

Another dramatic paused. They are both so very
uncomfortable, there is an invisible cloud looming over
both of them.

                    FLIGHT ATTENDANT
                 (over the intercom)
We will now begin boarding for our
first class passengers and those
requiring any special assistance
boarding....

                    ELIZABETH
                 (standing up, gripping her
                 carry on luggage)
So this is it....

John stares down hard and stops his feet from moving.

                    JOHN
                 (almost whispering)
Don't go.

                    ELIZABETH
What?

                    JOHN
                 (with more conviction)
I said "Don't go".

ELIZABETH
John....

JOHN
Listen to me.
    (stands up and looks her in
    the eye)
I know we agreed that it was best to
let this just be the week. Well, nine
days and seven hours, but still.

ELIZABETH
John, I can't....

JOHN
I know what you're thinking. You're
thinking "I can't stay here. We barely
know each other. I have a life back in
Boston. There's so much I have to do."
But, fuck all that!

ELIZABETH
John, we both know...

JOHN
What? What do we know? I don't know
anything. Ask anyone. They'll tell you.

ELIZABETH
This is insane. I can't just stay, no
matter how I feel.

JOHN
How do you feel? Tell me.

                    ELIZABETH
You know...

                       JOHN
Say it.

                 FLIGHT ATTENDANT
                  (over the intercom)
We will now begin general boarding,
rows fifty through thirty.

                    ELIZABETH
My gut is telling me to stay. Common
sense says I should get on this plane
and pretend I don't know this crazy
person out here, but there's something
else.....
      (she gulps hard and closes
      her eyes)
Every fiber of my being is saying
"Stay. stay here." With every part of
me that doesn't listen to common sense.

She opens her eyes.

                       JOHN
                  (in a near panic)
I like your gut, and I'm not just
talking about your washboard belly.
Listen, I pretended this moment was
never gonna come. I pretended like I
could let you go without saying a word.
I can't. My heart is screaming out of
my chest.

He grabs her by the waist and kisses her passionately.

BACK OFFICE

She drops her carry on bag.

FLIGHT ATTENDANT
(over the intercom)
We are now seating rows twenty nine
through ten.

Their kiss draws a lot of attention as people stnad and
walk past trying to get on the plane.

C.U. of their faces as the kiss fades. John's eyes are
still closed, and Elizabeth looks to the ground and
sinks into a hug with him.

ELIZABETH
I have to go.

She can't let go of him. He can't let go of her. The
line moves in Slow Motion behind them, people filing
into the plane, until there us no one left but them

FLIGHT ATTENDANT
(over the intercom)
Final boarding for flight 3055 non stop
service to Boston.
(out of the microphone and
yelling at Elizabeth)
That means you!

Elizabeth strains as she breaks off from John. He looks
as if he cannot stand up, like his life line has been
cut.

As Elizabeth reaches the gate, she turns and faces John,
tears in her eyes. She blows him a kiss and waves
goodbye.

After the door closes on her. He blows a kiss back to
her.

JOHN
Goodbye, Elizabeth.

INT. TERMINAL HALL BETWEEN GATES -   NIGHT

John walks slowly by. Head hung low. People pass by and
the crowd scarcely notices him in the hustle. A large
man bumps into John.

LARGE MAN
Excuse me there fellah.

John doesn't even notice or look up.

EXT. AIRPORT TERMINAL DROP OFF - NIGHT

This is where all the taxi's and cars are dropping off
and picking up people.

John stops at the curb, and fumbles for his keys, looks
up and waits for an opening in the traffic to walk
across to the parking garage.

INT. TERMINAL HALL BETWEEN GATES - NIGHT

Elizabeth runs through the crowd of people in the same
direction as John had before. She is running at top
speed and bumping people as she goes without
apologizing.

EXT. AIRPORT TERMINAL DROP OFF - NIGHT

An opening come up and John starts across. He jogs
slightly and gets to the opposite side.

                    ELIZABETH
               (Off Camera, over the bustle
                of the car honking and noise)
               John! John!

John looks around in a surprise. It's too good to be
true. He scans the parked cars for the voice.

                    ELIZABETH
               John! John!

He spots her and sees her waving.

                    JOHN
               Elizabeth!

John runs toward her in the mass of cars and tries to
get to her.

Elizabeth leaves the curb and runs to him also.

  Just as they are about four feet from one another, arms
  outstretched...

  A yellow Cab honks its horn loudly.

  They grab hold of one another and he swings her around
  full circle.

                              FADE TO BLACK :

FRIEND OR FOE?

One of my biggest filmmaking and screenwriting influences is Neil Labute, as well as Kevin Smith. The premise here was to make compelling characters who are complete opposites that are lifelong friends. This was before I really learned that film is a "show me" medium not a "tell me medium". The goal was to still attempting to make the audience care about two characters and the conflict between them.

EXT. 747 AIRLINER OVER AN OCEAN - DUSK

A generic, plane over a sea of clouds in the purple sky.

INT. 747 SEATS 21A AND 21B - DUSK

This the last leg of a long flight. It is not full and some people are spread out.

Sitting in their seats are RICK NELSON, 22 with nose ring and poorly dyed blonde hair, that's a near peroxide white than blonde. Next to him is DAVE SUMNER, 23 and with brown hair that is unkept and spiky after trying to sleep on this long transatlantic flight.

DAVE is covered by an airline blanket and one of the tiny pillows is falling out from beneath him. It hits the ground and he wakes up. RICK is awake and holding an empty plastic cup with the remnants of a cocktail.

                    DAVE
                  (groggy)
              I hate sleeping on these planes. You
              can never get comfortable. And what in
              the hell are these?

BACK OFFICE

(holds up the tiny pillow &
undersize blanket)
I mean, these are made for midgets.

RICK
It's not P.C. to say midget now. It's
"little Person". I couldn't sleep
anyway.

DAVE
Why, did the martini not do
it for you?

RICK
It was fine.

DAVE
How can you drink that airline piss?

A flight attendant passes by.

DAVE
(to the stewardess)
Hey, missy. I know we're not in first
class, but can you get me and my friend
here a refill?

FLIGHT ATTENDANT
(with the usual fake smile
and charm)
I'm sorry, sir, but the beverage cart
has already been by.

DAVE
I know the beverage cart has been by,
but I was asleep. I missed it.

                    FLIGHT ATTENDANT
              (still with a full smile)
          It is our policy not wake our guests
          while they are sleeping.

                    DAVE
          I paid for a drink. Can I please have a
          drink.

                    FLIGHT ATTENDANT
          I'm sorry sir.

Dave signals for her to move in closer. She leans into
him, as if she's going to hear a secret..

                    DAVE
              (shouting)
          No, it doesn't look infected, but my
          God! Stop scratching it. Make an
          appointment and we'll get a better look
          at it.

The flight attendant is dumbfounded, and confused.
People are stirred by the uproar, and staring.

                    DAVE
          Does your husband know? Genital herpes
          is not a laughing matter.

The Flight attendant looks back at Dave with contempt.
Then as everyone else on the plane stares at her, she
moves on.
                    RICK
          Jumping Jesus on a pogo stick, will you
          please shut up?

BACK OFFICE

Dave smiles and settles back in his seat, triumphant.

DAVE

You see? You just got to show these broads who's boss.

Rick is smiling with his eyes closed.

DAVE

What in the hell are you doing? Meditating?

RICK

I'm just... content.

DAVE

With what this shitty second class seating on a transatlantic flight? Maybe you've had too many martini's.

RICK

No, I'm content with life.

DAVE

Why? Life sucks.

RICK

Why would you say your life sucks?

DAVE

No, YOU'RE life sucks, not mine.

RICK

Oh. I don't think my life sucks.

DAVE
Why not? Think about this. You land
your first big job, and before you can
even get a few bucks in the 401K, you
get laid off due to a merger. You've
got no prospects and a skimpy resume.

RICK
Neither do you.

DAVE
I'm rich I don't need a job. HELLO!

RICK
I'm still pretty happy.

DAVE
Why? Europe is behind us and the
depravity of a desolate, mundane future
is staring at us in forty five minutes
when this plane lands at JFK
international. That does not sound like
a solid reason to be happy.

RICK
I'm still happy. I've got Lena.

DAVE
I don't know how to tell you this, but
you don't have Lena. She stayed in
Prague, and you left. I'd say that
nullifies your theory.

RICK
Lena and I will have this bond between
us forever.

BACK OFFICE

DAVE
Oh for Christ's sake.

Dave rolls over and tries to close his eyes to this.

RICK
I mean it. I'll never be the same and I
am forever changed because of her.
There was chemistry, there was love,
there was....

DAVE
.... my airline dinner coming back up
for the vomit bag.

RICK
Why are you always so cynical?

DAVE
(from his head turned the
other direction
Because when the world screws me over,
I'm a lot more prepared for it.

RICK
I used to be like you. I thought I'd
never love again. I thought this was
it. I'm twenty two and already set for
the celibacy.
(eyes look out toward the
window)
Lena changed all that. I would climb
mountains for her, cross oceans for
her. I want to write poems for her, and
make sculptures in her honor.

                DAVE
Dude, I can't even get you to pick up
your clothes off the floor and you want
to write her fucking poems.

                RICK
Have you ever had a woman make you feel
like that.

                DAVE
        (trying to suffocate himself
        with the tiny pillow)
Of course I have. Then I smack her on
the ass and tell her to make my
breakfast.

                RICK
You have never been in love.

                DAVE
You do realize I had sex with Lena,
right?

                RICK
What?!?

                DAVE
Come on, you had to know.

                RICK
You did not.

                DAVE
Rick, everyone had sex with her.

RICK
I never had sex with her!

DAVE
Yeah, I know, that was a real shame
too. I mean did you see her ass?

RICK
How could you do this to me?

DAVE
I was doing it to her, not you, Dave.
And believe me, she was more than
willing. It was her idea.

RICK
When? When did this happen?

DAVE
A couple times after hat night you went
for the long walk by the Danube river.

RICK
(very irritated)
That was the night we met, you prick.

DAVE
Hey, you were out buying her flowers or
some shit, then she came in my room and
we just kinda did it, you know? How
could you not know? She was covered
with sweat. And that was not hand
lotion she had in her hands.

> RICK
> (shaking he's so angry)
> You are a very sick man, did you know
> that?

> DAVE
> (still trying to close his
> eyes and sleep)
> So I've been told.

> RICK
> How could you do this to me? I mean
> didn't you feel any regret? I just
> want to know why. Why did you do it?

Dave rolls back over, obviously he can't sleep through this.

> DAVE
> Of course I felt a little guilty. I
> mean I thought of you the whole time.

> RICK
> (confused)
> What do you mean?

> DAVE
> I kept thinking to myself as I smacked
> her ass and made her squeal, "Rick
> could be doing this exact thing instead
> of me of only he'd get rid of that halo
> over his head."

> RICK

BACK OFFICE

This is typical Dave. You've always ben like this. Ever since we were kids. Do you remember our senior year?

> DAVE
> Not the Rebecca incident again.

> RICK
> Do you remember?

> DAVE
> I remember that YOU said you didn't have a rubber.

> RICK
> Just because you had one, I meant I wanted you to give it to me, not have sex with my prom date.

> DAVE
> If you had been a good boy scout and brought your own you could have been right there instead of me. Always be prepared.

> RICK
> Just go play hide and go fuck yourself, okay?

> DAVE
> Do you really think women go for sensitivity? Really? I mean I treat people like shit and I get more ass than dyke at Lilith Fair.

Rick picks up one of the airline phones and dials a

39

number.

> RICK
> Who are you calling?

> DAVE
> I have to check my voice mail.

> RICK
> Great.

> VOICE MAIL
> ... I know you met Roger at the National Training last year, so I thought you'd get a kick out of that. Anyway, I was just coming out of the meeting and I was thinking, God, I loved giving it to you from behind...

> DAVE
> (hands the phone over to Rick)
> Listen to this.

> RICK
> What is it?

> DAVE
> Just listen.

> VOICE MAIL
> ... You were so good. I loved being inside of you. I can't wait until next week when I get to come back to town and we can get together again. You did things to me that I've never had done.

BACK OFFICE

The plane starts to descend very fast. The oxygen masks drop
and the fasten seat belt signs go on.

RICK
What the hell is going on?

DAVE
We're going down!

FADE TO BLACK :

SOUND FX: Emergency alarms start blaring, people scream,
the engines dies off, and the sound of the air pressure
dropping is heard.

FLIGHT ATTENDANT
(over the intercom)
We are going down! Everyone please
stay calm! Oh my God ....

The sound fades out as the sounds of panic continue.

THE QUARRY

*The goal with this script was to make an action/chase story,
that was more visual than dialogue heavy. The intent was to
shoot in New York or any other big city with a subway. When I
made this myself, I changed the locale to a parking garage
because we have no rail system in Columbus Ohio. The
adaptability of any of the scripts is in the execution of it and can
become whatever you imagine. Eveyr problem is a creative
opportunity to solve.*

EXT. DOWNTOWN STREET - DAY

The usual uptight, GQ men and women walking around in
the $800 suits and cell phones wander aimlessly like
rats in a maze.

From outside an upscale hair salon comes out NOEL
WILSON, 31 and very tan. His new haircut is short, but
longer bangs. He has very expensive glasses on. His cell
phone rings and he pulls it out of his suit jacket.

                    NOEL
          Hello? ... No, I said Mr. Norton
          wanted to trade his Microsoft stock for
          Intel, not vice versa. I'll be back up
          in an hour...Yeah, I just go my
          haircut, so now I want to get some
          lunch.
               (checks his watch)
          I should be back on time for that job
          interview. If Sherry calls, let her
          know I'm running late...
               (pulls a little wedding ring
               box from his jacket)
          I've got it right here. I hope it's the
          right ring. She had a very specific cut
          of the diamonds she wanted... what's
          that? ... yes, I know i's a little
          superficial, but so am I. I'll talk to
          you after I Pop the big question. Bye.

Noel hangs up the phone and puts it inside his jacket.

BACK OFFICE

EXT. CORNER OF WALL ST AND AN ALLEYWAY - DAY

Noel walks by a hot dog vendor, he walks to the front of
the line. There are at least ten people waiting.

> NOEL
>
> Shit!
> (checks his watch)
> Excuse me.

> HOTDOG VENDOR
>
> Hey, back of the line asshole!

> NOEL
>
> I just need to know, does this alley
> come out by the subway station on 79th
> street.

> HOTDOG VENDOR
>
> Yeah, just keep going past the back of
> the First Bank, and turn right on 33rd.

> NOEL
>
> Thanks a lot.

Noel starts to walk down the alley way. It's dirty and
grimy, a homeless person is rooting through the garbage.

EXT. ALLEYWAY - DAY

Noel is walking very fast and trying to not run. He
stops when a sudden crash sound is heard in front of him
and behind a giant trash bin.

Noel quietly leans up to the trash bin and looks around

the side.

There are two men in cheap suits, and a bit overweight looming over a JUNKIE (SHITBAG). The first man in a suit, DETECTIVE BENJAMIN, 36 and oily black hair, is holding SHITBAG by the neck and directing his frail body back and forth. DETECTIVE JEROME, 42 even more overweight and salt and pepper hair, just stands idly by and watches with little interest.

                    DETECTIVE BENJAMIN
          I think this piece of shit wants to
          tell us something, Jerome. Is that
          right shitbag?

                    SHITBAG
          I ain't got nothing more to say without
          my lawyer.

                    DETECTIVE BENJAMIN
          (slams him headfirst into the
          metal side of the garbage
          bin)
          Funny man.

                    DETECTIVE JEROME
          I think he might have a change of heart
          coming soon, there Benji. I just don't
          think he understands the velocity of
          his situation.

                    DETECTIVE BENJAMIN
          What the hell does that mean?

                    DETECTIVE JEROME
          Just hit him again.

BACK OFFICE

Benjamin picks the bleeding junkie up from the ground
and then kicks him in the gut.

Noel watches this form around the corner. He can clearly
see the undercover policemen's badges around their
necks.

                    SHITBAG
          Okay, here it is, here it is.

He hands them a small baggie.

                    DETECTIVE JEROME
          But that's not all, is it? If my
          psychotic nature tells me...

                    DETECTIVE BENJAMIN
          That's psychic nature.

                    DETECTIVE JEROME
          Shut up, your making me look bag in
          front of the junkies. As I was saying,
          my psychic nature tells me that you
          also have a key to a safe deposit box.

SHITBAG hands him a key with a shaky hand.

After Benjamin takes it, Jerome steps up, un holsters
his 9mm with a silencer from inside his jacket and with
a quick move, shoots SHITBAG in the head.

Noel leans back against the dumpster. His cell phone
starts to ring.

                    DETECTIVE BENJAMIN

What the fuck is that?

Noel takes out the phone and tries to shut it off.

                    DETECTIVE JEROME
          Somebody's right there.

                    NOEL
          (drops the phone to the
          ground)
          Shit!

Noel bolts past the two detectives.

                    DETECTIVE JEROME
          Get the son of a bitch!

The two cops run after him.

EXT. CORNER OF WALL ST AND AN ALLEYWAY - DAY

     Noel, covered in sweat, runs past the people walking to
     and fro. He looks back over his shoulder.

     The two Detectives are not far behind.

     Noel looks left and right, there is an entrance to a
     subway station and he bolts down the stairs.

INT. SUBWAY STATION - DAY

     Noel jumps over the railing.

     He gets to the bottom just in time to see a train

leaving the station. Now there are only a few stragglers in the station now.

                    NOEL
          Shit.
               (looking around)
          Shit!

The sound of the detectives running down the steps is heard. Noel hides behind one of the girders that acts as a post.

                    DETECTIVE BENJAMIN
          Did he make the train?

                    DETECTIVE JEROME
          I don't think so.

                    DETECTIVE BENJAMIN
          Spread out, let's check it out.
               (to a few people, flashing
               his badge)
          Police business, everybody evacuate
          this station.

                    DETECTIVE JEROME
          NOW!

The few people left in the station leave in a hurry when the detectives take out their guns.

Noel is sweating and clenching his fists. Slowly checking all the nooks and crannies are the two detectives.

> DETECTIVE BENJAMIN
> Hey there little camper. Do us a favor
> and just come out and play.

> DETECTIVE JEROME
> Yeah pretty boy. Just show us your
> face.

A Wino stumbles over an ignores the cops and walks by talking to himself. He sees Noel and stares at him a long moment. Noel makes the sign for "Shhh".

Benjamin sees the Wino staring. He walks straight toward the post where Noel is hiding. As he gets within ten feet of the post, the Wino runs away. Benjamin steps on a broken bottle and the crackle is very loud. He stops in his tracks.

Noel hears this and he bends both his knees. He reaches on the ground to the trash can in front of him.

Benjamin continues on forward very slowly.

Noel pulls out a bottle from the trash can, also slowly and very quietly.

Benjamin stops next to the post. He listens intently for any kind of sign that someone is there.

Noel is still down low, he turns his head as he hears breathing. Noel holds his breath.

Noel jumps out and hits Benjamin on the head with the bottle. It smashes and the gun goes off, reverberating in the tunnel.

Noel makes a mad dash to the stairs leading out of the

subway.

                    DETECTIVE JEROME
                      (Off Camera)
                Benji, are you okay?
                      (to Noel)
                You cock sucker, I'm gonna get you.

 Noel flies up the stairs.

EXT. WALL STREET - DAY

Noel runs forward, his expensive suit ruined and he is covered in grime and sweat.

Noel runs around a corner and looks over to the subway exit. No one comes out. He turns back around the corner and breathes a sigh of relief.
                      NOEL
                  (under his breath)
                Thank God.

He sees the whole world is normal, although he is evoking stares from people passing by. He even starts to laugh.

Just as he starts to walk off, Jerome appears behind Noel, silencing his panting.

Noel is smiling as he stops, sensing something. Before he even turns around, Jerome fires his gun at him.

                    DETECTIVE JEROME
                Freeze! I said freeze!

Jerome puts three more bullets into Noel. Noel's chest is covered in blood. He sees the red on his fingers and closes his eyes. Jerome drops the baggie of drugs from SHITBAG on Noel's chest.

FADE TO BLACK :

DETECTIVE JEROME
(Off Camera)
I need an ambulance on the corner of
Wall Street and 94th street. I have a
homicide. It's apparently a drug deal
gone bad.

The sound fades to nothing as the sirens roar.

THE JOB INTERVIEW

The humor of THE JOB INTERVIEW was meant to evoke the stylings of Ally McBeal or more of a sitcom TV style of humor. The light hearted, aloof protagonist attempting to continue to get unemployment was my hero. In the end, I edited out over 70% of the screenplay that was shot because of both performance issues and also because of direction by me. Not every joke is funny, and sometimes you can overplay the humor.

INT. CONFERENCE ROOM - DAY

There is a long wooden table. Here sits JANE WATSON, late 30's the Interviewer, and MICHAEL COX, early 20's and the Interviewee.

Jane is on the phone and Michael is looking about the room, rather lazily.

BACK OFFICE

JANE
(into the phone)
Yes, well if Noel comes in, please send
him to conference room S immediately.
Thank you.
(hangs up receiver)
Mr. Wilson will be unable to join us
for the interview.

MICHAEL
That's okay. I have no idea who that
is.

Jane is completely monotone and has zero personality and even
less emotion throughout the entire process. She begins to open a
manilla folder containing Michael's file.

JANE
I have here your file.

MICHAEL
(hold up a legal pad)
And I have here a legal pad.

JANE
Interesting...

MICHAEL
Isn't it? I grabbed it from the supply
closet.

JANE
Let's begin shall we?

MICHAEL

We shan't.

                    JANE
Excuse me?

                    MICHAEL
Nothing.

                    JANE
Desired position?

                    MICHAEL
Reclining. Ha ha, no I am applying for
the marketing position.

Jane writes on a sheet of paper.

                    JANE
Desired salary?

                    MICHAEL
$125,000 a year complete with annual
bonuses and an office the likes of
which Michael Eisner has only dreamed.

Jane writes on a sheet of paper.

                    MICHAEL
But I'll take $34,000 a year and a
cubicle.

Jane writes on a sheet of paper.

                    JANE
Education?

BACK OFFICE

MICHAEL
Yes.

JANE
Last position held?

MICHAEL
Target for middle management hostility.

JANE
Salary?

MICHAEL
Less than slave wages with small
incentives to commit suicide.

JANE
Most notable achievement?

MICHAEL
My incredible collection of Star Wars
action figures.

JANE
Reason for leaving last position.

MICHAEL
Once they stopped paying me, the
passion for the work just faded away.

JANE
If you were to work here, what would
your preferred schedule be?

MICHAEL
1:30 to 3:30 on Mondays, Tuesdays, and
Thursdays.

Jane writes on a sheet of paper.

MICHAEL
But, I think I can free up my schedule
to allow me to work 8 to 5 Monday
through Friday.

Jane scratches off what she wrote on the notepad.

JANE
Do you have any special skills?

MICHAEL
Yes, but they're better suited to a
more intimate setting.

JANE
May we contact your current employer?

MICHAEL
You're talking to him now, did you me
to give myself a sterling
reccomendation?

And Jane writes more down on her pad.

JANE
Do you have any inhibiting physical
conditions that would prevent you from
lifting thirty pounds or more?

MICHAEL
Of what? This is an office.

Jane writes on a sheet of paper.

JANE
Have you received any special awards or
accomodations?

MICHAEL
I may already be a winner in the
publishers clearinghouse sweepstakes.
    (holds up fingers, crossed)
 Cross your fingers for me.

JANE
Do you smoke?

MICHAEL
Only when set on fire.

JANE
Where do you want to be in five years?

MICHAEL
Ah, living in Barcelona with a
beautiful leggy model type woman who
doesn't speak English on my arms, while
I write poetry and paint fresco's.

Jane writes on a sheet of paper.

MICHAEL
Actually, I don't have to wait five
years, do I? I'd like to get started

on that Barcelona thing right away.

Jane writes for a much longer period this time.

                    JANE
Well Michael, I think this should
conclude our interview.

                  MICHAEL
Gee thanks, I feel I know you so well
now. I feel as though you really opened
up in today's session. Next week, We'll
see how you feel about me telling you
some more about myself.

                    JANE
I think you will make a significant
member of the team.

                  MICHAEL
Excuse me?

                    JANE
You've got the job. HR will contact you
about salary, but I do hope that is
negotiable.

                  MICHAEL
Thank you, may I see what you wrote on
your notepad?
          (reaches for the notepad)
I have to ask, how in the hell did I
manage to get this job?

                    JANE
          (rips the notepad away from

him)
Marketing involves creativity and you
seem to have an over abundance.

They both stand up.

JANE
Have a great day.

MICHAEL
Setting the bar a little high, there
aren't you?

She stares at him blankly.

MICHAEL
I w as just going to have a normal day,
now I feel all this pressure to try to
do something extraordinary, like climb
a mountain or sky dive. Why not just
say "Have a normal day."?

JANE
Goodbye.

She exits the room.

These were among some of the first shorts I had ever written. My sole experience was writing feature length screenplays. Several of these were originally commissioned by someone at Tribeca Film, but the project never materialized, so they were adapted to these scripts to be the first things I would write and direct, as well as produce, which I did in January through March of 2000.

2

PASS THE SALT

PASS THE SALT represents another screenplay that combines four stories in one. I had some minor success with the previous segment FRIEND OR FOE and enjoyed working with the two improvisational actors, George Caleodis and Joe Teeters, that I revived their "characters" for this piece. In the end, the 4th story remains unproduced to this day. I felt I had done too many movies that were light on plot and heavy on "pop culture" reference.

INT. DINER TABLE ONE - DAY

It's a greasy spoon, and a few of the tables have people at it. Sitting at one table is PAUL, JACK, and his buddy CHRIS. Paul is chain smoking and talking. Chris is reading a book.

JACK
I don't buy into that. I don't think
that the producers intentionally killed
Brandon Lee so that the Crow would make
more money.

PAUL
Think about it. Was the movie really
all that good?

CHRIS
    (eyes never leaving the
    book)
I liked it.

PAUL
See my point? Brandon Lee hadn't done
a movie that made money. This was NOT a
sure thing. The movie would have bombed
had it not been for the mystique of
seeing some dead guy playinga dead on
screen.

JACK
I still don't buy it.

PAUL
The producers weren't doing well at all
at this point. They were desperate for
a hit financially.

CHRIS
    (eyes never leave the book)
I thought the girl who played the dead
girlfriend was pretty cute.

PAUL
    (ignoring Chris)
Let me put it to you this way. Would
you believe that some guy would kill
someone else for a million dollars?
You'd believe that right. That someone

who normally wouldn't kill WOULD kill
for one million dollars cash?

                    JACK
Yeah, of course.

                    PAUL
Well, the producers made over ten
million dollars, and continue to make
millions each straight to video crappy
sequel gets made. Maybe I'm paranoid.
Maybe I'm not. But, don't you think
safety is a major issue on a real movie
set?

                    CHRIS
          (eyes never leave the book)
The last one had Kirsten Dunst. She's
cute.

                    JACK
Dude, shut up.

                    VOICE (O.C.)
Can you pass the salt?

One table over, RICK reaches over and grabs the
salt shaker from Chris.

INT. DINER TABLE TWO - DAY

RICK puts salt on his fries. DAVE (George) stares off
to the wall.

                    RICK

So she never turns in her work. I mean
she's a menace to the office. She's
always late, she pawns off her work to
Larry, and magically, she never gets
fired.

                DAVE
What do you care?

                RICK
It's not right.

                DAVE
It's not even your department. What
does this have to do with you?

                RICK
I work very hard, and she's always
coming late from whatever medical
problem of the week she's ranting about
and... I guess it's just indicative of
all thing wrong in Corporate America,
that's all.

Dave takes a long drag off his cigarette.

                DAVE
Look at Scooby Doo. You think this is a
show for kids?

                RICK
Of course it is. Scooby Doo. It's a
cartoon.

                DAVE
Yeah right. You've got four high school

kids in the sixties that never go to
school, never hold down jobs, and never
see their parents. All they ever do is
drive around in that hippie van called
the "Mystery Machine". This show is
really about rampant drug abuse. Shaggy
is so stoned that he eats the dog
snacks. They all drop acid and start
seeing ghosts. Of course Fred and
Daphne go to search upstairs in the
bedroom to get it on. That leaves Velma
& Shaggy to go chasing vapor trails.
Velma is so high she can't see anything
without her glasses. Not to mention
that they all think the dog can speak
to them. These kids always get away
with breaking the law... ever heard of
trespassing? Did you ever notice that
the adults are also always portrayed as
bad guys? I mean, no parents, no
positive role model adults, and the
cops never give them a reward.

                    VOICE (O.C.)
Can you pass the salt?

DAVE hands the salt over to...

INT. DINER TABLE THREE - DAY

SANDY, early to mid 20's, grabs the salt from the other
table. Sandy sits at the table alone reading a newspaper.

                    SANDY

(to Dave)
Thanks.

DAVE (O.C.)
No problem, toots.

SANDY
Moron.

Then her friend ELLIE, or EL as her friends call her, also early to mid 20's, sits down with her.

EL
Sorry I'm late. What's up?

Tosses her purse into the booth.

SANDY
I'm just really tired. I was at work late last night. We had those files to box up for the annual annuity reports.

EL
What is your title in your department now?

SANDY
"Relationship Banker."

EL
Relationship Banker? What is that? I mean, do you setup mutual funds for couples and then have the stock market do analysis on their relationships?

                SANDY
I for one believe that relationships
should be more like the stock market.
There were several guys I wish had left
me with a severance package.
    (pause to sip coffee)
So did you go out with the new guy in
Accounts Receivables?

                EL
Yeah. We went out...
    (she cringes a little)

                SANDY
Well?

                EL
I don't know. He was too sensitive.

                SANDY
What do you mean too sensitive?

                EL
He was too nice, you know? There is
such a thing as TOO nice. I need to
have some degree of testosterone.

                SANDY
I don't get you. You complain that
there's no men, but then you trash
every guy we work with. Have you ever
considered going out with Kurt?

                EL

Kurt's a sweetie and all, but he
doesn't bode well on the Line of
Masculinity.

                SANDY
The "Line of Masculinity"?

                EL
Yeah. There's a graph.
        (gestures with her hands)
On the right we have the ultra
sensitive, whiny, Ross from Friends,
effeminate types. The extreme right is
a gay man.

We'll make a graphic of the actual LINE OF MASCULINITY,
so frame the shots accordingly.

                EL (CON'T)
On the extreme left are the really,
muscled headed idiots, that are total
insensitive idiots.

                SANDY
Okay.

                EL
So the guy last night is right about
here
        (points towards the right of
        the line)
He was so nice and sensitive, but there
was no animal attraction. And Kurt,
well Kurt unfortunately falls over here
        (points just left of center)
and Michael, well you remember what a

fiasco Michael is, right?

SANDY
Oh yeah, he falls in right over there
     (points to the extreme left)
He is about as sensitive as gas station
toilet paper.

EL
So we should aspire towards finding a
guy that's sensitive, but still
masculine. A guy who brings you
flowers, but still acts like a GUY.
     (points dead center)
That's what I want. There just doesn't
happen to be any.

SANDY
What about Sean Connery? He could be
dead center on the line.

EL
Oh yeah, Sean could be dead center. But
isn't he like eighty years old by now?
The Sean Connery from Goldfinger maybe,
but not now.

SANDY
I don't care how old Sean Connery is.
He is hot. Now there is a guy that
could never be gay.

EL
Any man could be gay. You can't tell.

SANDY

Sean Connery could never be gay. He is the epitome of what every heterosexual man should aspire to be.

FADE TO BLACK:

INT. HOUSE, OUTSIDE BATHROOM - NIGHT

There is a party going on (music blaring), and RICK and DAVE are waiting to use the bathroom.

                    DAVE
          (banging on the door)
           Come on, already.

                    RICK
          Dave, don't do that.

                    DAVE
          Why not?

                    RICK
          I know if I were taking a dump, I
          wouldn't want someone banging on the
          door. It might cause whoever it is to
          pinch.

                    DAVE
             (banging again)
          Hurry up.
             (stops)
          Oh, I watched those tapes you loaned
          me. I did all eight minutes, and
          still... nothing. I think that's a
          ripoff. Eight minute abs my ass.

RICK

I think you're supposed to use them for
more than just eight minutes. Maybe
eight minutes a day.

DAVE

That's intentional misdirection. I feel
violated.

RICK

You know, just because no one
understands you, does NOT make you an
artist.

DAVE

You're validating my inherent mistrust
in friendship.
    (bangs on the door again)
This is the only bathroom in the whole
house. Come on.

RICK

Stop it. It's rude.

DAVE

I'll stop being rude if you stop being
retarded.

RICK

I don't know what your problem is, but
I'll bet it's hard to pronounce.

Looking at a PEANUTS cartoon on the wall.

DAVE
How long will they keep printing this crap?

RICK
What? Charlie Brown? Forever. Charles Schultz was way more advanced than people give him credit for.

DAVE
What do you mean?

RICK
Modern relationships were pretty well covered. Charlie Brown is obviously gay and in love with Linus who has this bizarre blanket fetish. Look at how Charlie Brown is always after the red headed girl. Her constant snubbing of him eventually sends him down a spiral of self doubt that eventually leads him to homosexuality. Then there's the lesbian relationship between the ultimate tom boy Peppermint Patty and Marcy. Marcy is always calling her "Sir" because Peppermint Patty is the butch of the couple.

DAVE
The really complex relationship was always Schroder and Lucy. That's my kind of women. She would get all violent and dominatrix on him whenever he wouldn't pay attention.

FADE OUT

The middle section became the only script I have ever re-shot from scratch. Later, working with actors from The Second City cast, I had a chance to work with actors of a higher caliber and we remade this script as a short called THE LINE OF MASCULINITY. That short became one of my most watched pieces on the Internet with well over 1 million views combined from the various websites.

3

SNOW

This remains one of the very few short screenplays I have never produced. It was meant to be an excersize in visual storytelling, with minimal, if any dialogue. There were voice overs written, that I may not have intended to use in the edit, dependingon how clear the overall story was going to be. It remains intentionally vague as to what the "it" is. I wanted the audience to answer whether it was in his imagination or was it a real creature.

EXT. SNOW COVERED HILLS - DAY

As far as the eye can see, nothing but dunes of virgin snow. No footprints, nor any people.

The wind blows, the blue sky is a stark contrast to the pure white ground.

EXT. BACKYARD - DAY
We hear the muffled wound of children laughing. There are no words, just the flashback of emotion that is bliss.

ENTER TWIN BOYS, both are about eight years old, wearing glasses & a little too much winter dressing that makestheir movements a little awkward. They run in SLOW MOTION and they chase each other. Snow balls fly at one another.

EXT. SNOW COVERED HILLS - DAY

We pan forward through the snow

EXT. BACKYARD - DAY

The twins make a snow man. They push each piece of snow into a larger ball until the torso is complete.

EXT. CABIN, NEAR BEAR LAKE CANADA - DAY

A quaint, non electric cabin in the middle of the Yukon. Trees and snow surround the place. It looks as though this could actually be the 18th century or anytime when life was simpler.

                              MAN
                             (V.O.)
                    I came here to die. After the divorce,
                    I felt I had nothing left to offer
                    life.

INT. CABIN, NEAR FIREPLACE - DAY

MAN, late 20's, wearing glasses and wearing jeans and a sweater, sits before the fireplace. He is looking at a wedding picture.

                         MAN (V.O.)
                    I packed my bags, left the University

where I taught paleontology, and came
as far North as any white man has gone.
I'm in the middle of the Yukon. There
are no people, only the wild, and
what's left of the uninhabited world.

The Man wells up in his eyes as he looks at the photos.

EXT. CABIN, NEAR BEAR LAKE CANADA - DAY

The Man is chopping wood outside.

                    MAN (V.O.)
There is only so much tragedy one can
endure in a lifetime. My twin brother
died when I was eight. My father died
when I was seventeen and mother mother
and I were never what you might call
close.

INT. CABIN, NEAR FIREPLACE - NIGHT

Man is reading a book.

                    MAN (V.O.)
It's only a matter of time. I have no
allusions about the future.

EXT. FOREST - NIGHT

The trees are dark and ominous. Little is moving or
happening.

INT. CABIN, BEDROOM - NIGHT

The Man is suddenly thrust awake by a horrendous sound.

It's a combination of an animal or a person screaming and howling like a dog. The Man jumps out of bed. He goes to the window and stares out. He gets up and starts to get dressed.

EXT. CABIN, NEAR BEAR LAKE CANADA - NIGHT

The Man has a flashlight and starts out into the forest.

EXT. FOREST - NIGHT

In an eerie light, the Man sees that nothing is stirring, nothing is happening. He stares for a long moment ahead.

There is the silent vista of the valley. After he takes it in, he turns back and starts back.

EXT. CABIN, NEAR BEAR LAKE CANADA - DAY

The Man comes out the front door to the cabin. It is sunny out, but the snow is everywhere. The Man takes a long breath, then starts off into the forest.

EXT. FOREST - DAY

The man is walking along the creek. He has a stick in his hand. He looks to the ground as he walks. He suddenly stops and looks at the ground in detail

There are footprints in the snow. They are large, and there is red (blood) along the tracks.

The man looks ahead of them. The tracks lead off into the woods. He starts to follow after them.

EXT. POND, FOREST - DAY

The Man follows the tracks near a frozen pond. He watches the tracks go around into the woods again.

EXT. CLIFF SIDE, FOREST - DAY

The Man sees the creek run next to a small cliff. He sees the tracks and the blood trail lead into a small cavern.

Reluctantly, the Man enters the cave.

INT. CAVE - DAY

It is dark in the cave, but the Man cautiously and quietly enters.

There is a growling noise. The Man stops. The growls echo against the cave walls.

Even slower, the Man continues. As he gets deeper into the cavern, there is more sound. It sounds like bones being broken.

The Man sees ahead of him, the the VERY poorly lit cave, a brown, hairy creature (to be referred to as the BEAST).

It is too dark to make out if it is a person, a bear, Big Foot, or anything else. The Man tries to see it better, he squints in the dark. He cannot see very good.

The Man moves slightly closer. He slips on a rock and it makes a big noise in the cave.

The BEAST looks up. It roars like a lion.

The Man gets up and starts to bolt out of the cave. He

slips again.

The Beast closes in. The Man tries to get back up. Too late. The Beasts arm swings out at him. It hits him on the temple and he goes down.

FADE OUT:

EXT. BACKYARD - DAY

The twins play in the snow again. The snow man begins to crumble as the knock it over. One of the twins cries out.

The other looks on alone.

INT. CAVE - DAY

The Man starts to stir. He does not have his glasses on anymore and blood is streaming from his temple.

He looks around him. He is still in the cave, but not where he slipped. He is deeper in the cave. He looks a round him. There is no sign of the Beast. He scramble to his feet and starts out of the cave.

EXT. CLIFFSIDE, FOREST - DAY

The Man is running out of the cave, looking behind him to make sure that thing is not there. As he starts out into the woods, a roar from the beast is heard. The Man starts to run at a wider pace.

EXT. FOREST - DAY

The Man is running. He stops, out of breath and leans on a tree. He looks behind him. Nothing there. He looks ahead. He doesn't see the path he had come from, nor does he recognize the surroundings. Just as he starts to relax...

The Beasts long arm reaches around and almost takes his head off. It hits his shoulder instead. The Man had just started to lean down and the beast lets out another roar.

The Man starts to run again.

EXT. POND, FOREST - DAY

The Man runs across the creek near the pond. He is holding his arm in pain.

The Beast is trekking behind him. Only seen by its legs.

EXT. BRIDGE, NEAR CLIFF - DAY

The Man starts across an old fashioned bridge. He runs across.

The beast appears at the bridge as well.

The Man gets to the other side and sees that the Beast is still stalking him.

EXT. FOREST - DAY

The Man runs through the trees and snow.

The Beast continues after him.

At a crevise, the Man starts to climb through the foliage and rock to get to the top.

EXT. CLIFF SIDE, FOREST - DAY
The Man is at the bottom of a small cliff. He turns as a

roar is heard. Then the Man starts to climb the rock face. He tries to go faster, but the pain is too great.

He is above the halfway mark wehn the Beast begins to ascend as well.

The Man is pulling as hard as he can. His face is grim with pain and determination.

The Beast is climbing as well, shown only by the arm or legs at it ascends.

EXT. BACKYARD - DAY

The twins are playing near a small creek, on of the boys is hanging over the edge. The other is trying furiously to pull him back up. They both look terrified.

EXT. CLIFF SIDE, FOREST - DAY

The hand of the Man reaches the top of the cliff. He is trying to find something to hold on to.

EXT. BACKYARD - DAY

The grip of the twin on top is loosening.

EXT. CLIFF SIDE, FOREST - DAY

The Man is starting to slip as well.

EXT. BACKYARD - DAY

The twin over the edge falls down. The twin on top begins to cry.

EXT. CLIFF SIDE, FOREST - DAY

The Man pulls harder until he finally begins to pull himself up. He gets his torso over the edge of the cliff.

His face is a glow with relief.

Then the Beast roars. It is about to reach his feet. The Man pulls himself harder and harder until he is over the edge of the cliff.

EXT. BACKYARD - DAY

The twin looks down the side to see his brother. He sits alone in the snow. He is all alone in the yard. Playing alone. The snow man sits toppled over. The lone twin plays by himself.

EXT. CLIFF SIDE, FOREST - DAY

The man looks over the edge. There is nothing there. Nothing at all. The Man roll sover on his back. He sighs.

> MAN (VO)
> I came here to die. I found my reason
> to live.

FADE OUT:

In writing for what I had, at the time my twin nephews were 11 years old, so the intent of the flashbacks was to play on something I had access to – twins.

4

CONCUPISCENCE

I love the word Concupiscence because you have to look it up in a dictionary. The intent of the script was to deal with a form of sitcom style of writing, but with a twist ending. Again, being greatly affected by Joss Whedon's writing style, this was my own form of interpretation as an excersize in writing and directing.

INT. COPY CENTER - DAY

CUT BETWEEN Opening Credits print out on color copiers, laser printers, dot matrix printers.

ZOOM shots of extras working in a small copy shop downtown. WHIP PAN to & from the different people being described. (POV of Peter & Dan)

> DAN (V.O.)
> And what about her?

> PETER (V.O.)
> The impression I get is that she was
> the kinda girl in high school that was
> plain Jane, you know? One of those

girls that was never the homecoming
queen, but put together the dance.

DAN (V.O.)
I can see that. Always in all the clubs
and social, but never the girl every
guy wanted.

PETER (V.O.)
Right. And then in college she dated
one or two guys, married the long time
boyfriend. And now, she's in her late
twenties and fianlly blossomed into a
sexual creature and feels like she
missed something.

DAN (V.O.)
And her? She looks like she's had it
hard.

PETER (V.O.)
Mary? You know how some people get a
bit of the ugly tree? Someone made a
baseball bat and beat her senseless
with it.

DAN (V.O.)
You are truly evil, man.

PETER (V.O.)
I am an agent of the Devil, but my
duties are largely ceremonial. Now THIS
girl is something else.

C.U. (ZOOM) on BETSY, early 20's, dressed business like,
but very modern & sexy.

PETER (CON'T)
She has the look like a woman who is
repressing a latent desire, a woman who
is ready for discovery.

INT. COPY SHOP, DAN'S DESK - DAY

Two shot of DAN & PETER, early 30's, Dan is a little bit
disheveled, and Peter is very well dressed, but unshaven.

DAN
I think you're wrong. Betsy is right
out of college and my guess is she's
focussing on her career.

PETER
Yeah right. With those clothes? Are
you kidding me? She's in dire need of
man. Right out of college? She's
probably just getting over all of her
lesbian experiments with her roommate
in the dorm or with her sorority
sisters. Wearing those nighties and
possibly having a pillow fight with...

DAN
You ARE an idiot. Not every girl on
earth goes through a Penthouse Forum
story, you know.

PETER
Just look at her.

CUT TO: Show Betsy, arms folded, staring back at them.

CUT TO: back to the guys.

> PETER (CON'T)
> She could probably...

They slowly look back to her.

CUT TO: Betsy, eyebrow raised.

CUT TO: The guys start to straighten out their desks, and move around.

> DAN
> Maybe we should get back on that
> project file.

> PETER
> Do you have the invoice?

Betsy comes up to their desks.

> BETSY
> Don't you have work to keep you busy?

> DAN
> No, we were just...

> PETER
> It may not look like it, but on a
> molecular level, I am very busy. Can I
> ask you something?

Dan rolls his eyes.

> PETER (CON'T)

I was wondering if you could tell what
college you went to.

BETSY
I went to Bairdsford University.

PETER
Is that an all girl's school?

DAN
Peter...

PETER
It's just that, I think you are
attractive. I'm definitely attracted to
you. I think we should go out. You and
me.

BETSY
What's my last name?

PETER
Does it matter?

BETSY
It does to me.

PETER
I can always find out.

BETSY
If you were interested in something
other than just sex, you might have
thought to find that out.

PETER

What is your last name?

                    BETSY
BEFORE giving me a reason to mistrust
strangers.

                    PETER
I don't need to know your last name
when I cry out a name while giving you
a...

                    DAN
STOP!

                    BETSY
As much as I am refreshed and
challenged by your unique attempts,
you've got the emotional depth of a
rain puddle.

                    PETER
So maybe tonight at 8 O'clock?

                    BETSY
How about never? Does never work for
you?

INT. COPYSHOP, BOSSES OFFICE - DAY

The Boss, older and grumpy, comes out to the main room of
   the office.

                    BOSS
Can I please have everyone's attention?
This is important. We just received

word from our printers that all jobs
sent to them last night are lost. I am
looking for volunteers to work late
tonight to re-do the jobs.

Everyone gathers around the bosses office door. People
groan at the mention of overtime.

> PETER
Big boss man...

> BOSS
Peter, I'm visualizing the duct tape
over your mouth already.

> PETER
Sir, it's Friday night. Asking people
to work late like this is cruel and
unusual. I suggest our newest employees
put in the time. A lot of us have
already worked overtime in our tenure
here.

> BOSS
This idea actually sounds reasonable.
> (to his secretary)
Have the pharmacy refill my
prescription.

> PETER
If I might say, sir...

> BOSS
Do I have any volunteers?

> BETSY

I'll stay.

Dan perks up.

                    BOSS
Good. Anyone else?

                    DAN
I will too. It's a thankless job, but I
have a lot of bad karma to work off.

                    BOSS
Excellent. You'll both get some
overtime. Come into my office and I'll
divvy up the job assignments.

Everyone breaks off and goes back to work.

                    PETER
What are you doing? We're supposed to
go to Hooters tonight.

                    DAN
This is my chance. A night alone with
Betsy.

                    PETER
Chance? What chance? You have been
trying to hit on her for the last three
weeks.
        (frustrated sigh)
Need I remind you of the previous
attempts to even get a word out?

INT. BREAK ROOM, COPYSHOP - DAY

Flashback, BLACK & WHITE - film.

Betsy is going straight towards the refrigerator, and Dan moves in from the side. As he opens his mouth to speak, she slams him in the face with the freezer door.

INT. BREAK ROOM, COPYSHOP - DAY

Flashback, BLACK & WHITE - film

Betsy pours herself a cup of Java, and Dan pours coffee all over his hand as he tries to look calm. He starts to sweat and shiver as a 3rd degree burn sinks in. He runs off in a panic. Betsy looks at him crooked.

INT. COPYSHOP MAIN ROOM - DAY

Betsy sits at her desk. From behind, Dan tries to lean on her desk, and slips to the ground, but all the papers in his hands fly into the air.

INT. COPYSHOP MAIN ROOM - DAY

C.U. Dan & Peter, Dan staring into the bosses office.

Wide shot of window into bosses office, of Betsy getting her job assignment from the boss.

                    DAN
          Well, I was going to send her an email.
          That is the adult version of passing
          notes.

PETER
Are you insane? Give this up. Hooters.
Lots of them. And the food is good too.

DAN
Nope.

PETER
You leave me no choice. I am going to
have to help convince you.
(Dan rummages through his
desk)
Whenever there is a major decision in
my life, I have a technique that has
never lead me astray.
(finds it)
A-ha!

DAN
What is it?

Peter ceremoniously whips out a "Magic 8 Ball".

PETER
Will Dan find true love with Betsy
tonight?
(shakes the ball, reads it)
"Not likely". There is the proof. The
Magic 8 ball never lies.

DAN
It said "Not likely" which means there
is still a chance.

Dan starts to walk to the bosses office.

                              PETER
                    Don't say I didn't warn you.

                                                    FADE OUT:

INT. COPYSHOP MAIN ROOM - NIGHT

Wide shot, high up. MONTAGE sequence of Betsy and Dan
working in different places. Cross dissolve from place to
place. Working sometimes seperate, and sometimes together.

INT. COPYSHOP MAIN ROOM - NIGHT

At the plain copy machine, Betsy presses a button and turn
around.

                              DAN
                    Do you work out?

                              BETSY
                    Yeah. I go to the gym three times a
                    week. You?

                              DAN
                    I tried that 8 minute abs tape once,
                    but I did not get the six pack.

                              BETSY
                    I think you're supposed to use it more
                    than once.

                              DAN
                    I think that's misleading. It clearly
                    said "8 minute abs". I put in the 8
                    minutes. I let the Better Business
                    Bureau know how I felt.

BETSY
I'm going on a food run. Do you want
anything?

DAN
Sure. A hamburger. Medium.

BETSY
You like your burgers medium?

DAN
Yeah. Why?

BETSY
I've never known anyone else who gets
their burgers done medium.

DAN
I'm sure there are people who do.

BETSY
Well, yeah. DUH! I just mean, I've
never known anyone personally.

DAN
Thanks. Need some cash?

BETSY
I got this one, cowboy.

Betsy leaves.

INT. COPYSHOP, DAN'S DESK - NIGHT

Dan types into the computer and listens to music on his jam box.

The THEME FROM THE LOVE BOAT comes on. He turns up the volume. He stars to karaoke with it.

                                        CUT TO:

Overhead shot.

Dan is singing as Betsy enters and stares.

                BETSY
        I see you've set aside this time to
        humiliate yourself in public.

    Dan turns off the music.

                BETSY
        I don't know what your problem is, but
        I'm positive it's hard to pronounce.

                DAN
        Sorry. Sometimes you get a feeling, and
        you roll with it.

                BETSY
        The Love Boat?

                DAN
    Well...

Betsy sets down the bag of burgers.Dan moves towards her.

                DAN
        Can I tell you something?

                    BETSY
          Sure.

Dan leans next to her on the same desk.

                    DAN
          I don't know you that well, but I feel
          like I've known you forever. There's
          something about you, I can't put my
          finger on it. There's this connection.

He turns to her. She looks up at him.

                    DAN
          Maybe, I'm just crazy, but I have to
          tell you this. I think you are amazing.
          You are sweet. I see you giving "get
          well" cards to people you've worked
          with for less than a month. I can see
          your face light up when something goes
          your way. It's the way you get that
          look of triumph whenever finish your
          3:PM game of solitaire and win,
                (IMPROV LINES)
          You... are... perfect.

Dan leans in for a kiss. She closes her eyes too.

Just before their lips meet.

Betsy sucker punches Dan full swing into his stomach. Dan
crouches over, gasping for breath. Betsy stand upright.

BETSY
How stupid do you think I am?

DAN
(gasp)

BETSY
Take a sec. I see the picture of your
wife on your desk everyday.

DAN
(still gasping, not able to
fully stand up)

BETSY
Okay, I'm going back to work. Someday
we'll look back at this moment, laugh
nervously, and change the subject.

Betsy walks away. Dan's fingers are still on the desk, trying to
pull himself up.

FADE TO BLACK.

*The style can come across in a myriad of ways. You can
give the performances an "over the top" style or play it almost
dramatic and get two very different movies from the same script.*

5

LICENCE EXAM

This script fits an "altered reality" sketch style of writing. That's where something out of the ordinary is treated as the norm by the characters. This is a style of writing I enjoy and LINE OF MASCULINITY follows that style as well.

In particular, one of the most boring things and longest lines you face is at the Department of Motor Vehicles. I wrote this based on the soul crushing, agaonized faces of everyone waiting and working at the DMV on day.

INT. DMV OFFICE

Wide shot, show a line of people trying to get to the desk. Drab, florescent colours.

INT. DMV OFFICE

DMV DESK CLERK and GIRL CLERK look down as the current patrons walk off.

DMV DESK CLERK
Number 31, 32, and 33.

The next three patrons walk up to the counter, HARLEY,
HOLLY, and GEORGE.

The lights go dim, and an unseen announcer's voice
starts along with music.

ANOUNCER
Ladies and Gentlemen, the Department of
Motor Vehicles welcomes you to DRIVER'S
LISCENCE EXAM!

The DMV desk clerk turns around and hold a microphone

DMV DESK CLERK
Thank you! Let's meet out contestants.
Oh my, who is this young hottie.

Host kisses Holly on the cheek ala Family Feud.

HOLLY
My name is Holly, I'm a student at OSU
and I love bike riding and pets.

DMV DESK CLERK
Excellent. And you sir?

Host shakes hands with Harley.

HARLEY
My name is Harley, I work at First Bank
as an accounts manager.

DMV Clerk makes a THUMBS UP sign into the camera.

                DMV DESK CLERK
          (to George)
          And you sir?
          (before George can answer)

I'm sorry we have to move on. For the first question, Is
it legal to change lanes at an intersection.

Holly and Harley slam their hands down on counter.

                DMV DESK CLERK
          Holly.

                HOLLY
          No, it's not legal.

                DMV DESK CLERK
          That is correct!

Harley makes a frustrated look, George looks confused.

                GEORGE
          I didn't know we had a buzzer.

                DMV DESK CLERK
          Next question...If you are in the
          passing lane, should you pull over to
          the left side, or the right side?

Tock clicking sounds as the contestants think. Harley
buzzes in first.

                HARLEY
          Left?

BUZZER sound FX.

                    DMV DESK CLERK
          No.

George buzzes in.

                    GEORGE
          Ri....

Holly buzzes in.

                    HOLLY
          Right side?

                    DMV DESK CLERK
          That is correct.

George looks confused again.

                    DMV DESK CLERK
          Final question. Is it legal to park in
          a handicap spot that does not have a
          singpost?

                    HARLEY
          No.

                    DMV DESK CLERK
          I'm sorry that's incorrect.

                    GEORGE
          Yes, it's legal.

                    DMV DESK CLERK

Judges?

> HOLLY
> It is legal, but you shouldn't do it
> out of courtesy.

> DMV DESK CLERK
> Judges say, HOLLY IS THE WINNER!!!!

Confetti starts to fall, everyone claps. GIRL CLERK
hands Holly an oversized Drivers Lisence.

> DMV DESK CLERK
> We haven't forgotten our other
> contestants. Tell them what they win
> Chuck.

> ANOUNCER
> Well Jon, they just won A BRAND NEW
> BICYCLE! No liscence required!

Show a spotlight on a mountain bike.

The end.

6

BITTER OLD MAN

In the fall of 1999, I had been suffering from writer's block until I got a phone call from someone at Tribeca Film. They had read some feature script of mine and solicited me to write a series of short films where someone died at the end. I asked what they meant and he said "like two Japanese girls wearing Prada annoy people at a store, then walk outside and get hit by a cab."

From that, I wrote the first 8-9 short screenplays I had ever written. Three of these became a part of BACK OFFICE (chapter One), like THE QUARRY, ASPHYXIATED HEART, and FRIEND OR FOE, some with their original death endings, and others without. In the same 7 hour writing session came this script BITTER OLD MAN, and also MINIVAN (Chapter Seven).

BITTER OLD MAN deals with racism in a frank and hard way. In some ways it represents a progressive, modern form of racism wherein an old man can deal with black people, but the ugly predjudice comes out when it comes to marriage into his family.

INT. OLD APARTMENT IN THE BRONX - DAY

This is one o fthose ancient apartments with the layer of dust tht has been lying over everything since the Carter administration. ROBERT "BOB" LOY, 63 and balding, has a cigarette dangling from his lips, this too has been there since the Carter Administration. He sits under the window at his table. He wars and undershirt and boxers.

BOB
God damn this electric company.

Bob is wearing glasses near an inch thick and going through his bills on the table.

BOB (CONT'D)
Sons a bitches would charge
extra for the bullets that killed ya.

Bob walks into the kitchen. He grabs a bottle of Jack Daniel from on top of the refrigerator and a glass from the cupboard. Griping under his breath, he returns to the table and resumes his tirade.

The phone rings. Bob walks to the phone on a small table between the living room and kitchen.

BOB (CONT'D)
(very cranky)
Hello?

WILLIAM
(V.O. From phone)
Hey Pop, how ya doin'?

BOB

Well if it isn't my only daughter.

WILLIAM
Come on Pop, that was old
when I was twelve.

BOB
Maybe if ya'd gone and been
more of a man, I wouldn't call
you Mary.

WILLIAM
Pop, I know it's Sunday and all,
but I thought you'd like to come
over to my place for dinner tonight.

BOB
Is that nigger girlfriend of
yours gonna be there?

WILLIAM
(very angry)
Pop, don't call her that.

BOB
What's her name? Vagina?

WILLIAM
It's Virginia.

BOB
What the hell kinda name is
that for an African?

WILLIAM

Pop, we aren't having this conversation
again. I told you.
(pause)
Did you see the doctor this
week?

Bob lights up another cigarette and takes a long drag.

WILLIAM (CONT'D)
Are you there Pop?

BOB
Yea, I saw the doctor. He says
to me, "Bob, you gotta lay off
the sauce." He says it ain't no
good for me.

WILLIAM
And what did you say
to him?

BOB
I told him to bit my ass. I
was drinking whiskey by the bottle
before his parents were even
making baby batter in the
back of a pinto.

WILLIAM
Pop, he may be young, but he
went to school learn all this stuff
they're telling you. I'm worried
about you. You ain't been lookin'
too good lately.

BOB

Well, aren't you just a prissy
little girl.

WILLIAM
Okay, enough. Listen, are you
coming to dinner tonight or not.

BOB
Why is this so important? I got
a game of cards at Charlie's tonight.

WILLIAM
Well, I got something important
to tell everyone.

BOB
More important than winning
a hundred and fifty bucks form Charlie?

WILLIAM
I think so.

Long pause. Bob scratches himself

BOB
So what is it?

WILLIAM
Virginia and I are getting
married.

BOB
(explodes)
No you ain't.

WILLIAM

BITTER OLD MAN

I knew you were gonna
be like this, Pop.

BOB
What did you expect? You goin'
with some nigger is fine with me.
You wanna get your rocks off
with the monkeys, that's fine.
I donn't get it, but I'm okay, but you
will NOT marry some black
woman. If your mother were
alive today, she would...

WILLIAM
Leave Ma out of this.   Ma
would understand.

BOB
Oh no she wouldn't. Your mother
would have died of a heart attack at
the sight of you with one of them.
Sweet baby Jesus, Willie, I don't
believe you.

WILLIAM
Pop, this is just insane. I love her,
don't you get it?

BOB
And on a Sunday too. Don't you
have no respect of God?

WILLIAM
I love her, so what's wrong
with that?

BOB
Everything. It's just not right.
We ain't supposed to marry
them. It even says so in the bible.

WILLIAM
Is that the KKK version of the
bible, Pop? The book I read
said nothing about not marrying
someone you love.

BOB
You were always a stupid kid,
you know that? Always goin' and tryin'
to be different.

WILLIAM
Pop, it's important to me you
be there tonight, and be apart of this.

BOB
I want no part of this. I want no
part of you goin' and ruining
your life. What if you had kids,
huh? What about them? They'll be
outcasts, they'll be half breeds.

WILLIAM
Only to narrow minded fools
like you, Pop.

BOB
You're wrong.

Throws his glass of whiskey against the wall

BOB (CON'T)
You are not my son.
My son would never
do this to me. I don't know who
you are. No son of mine would
mix races.

WILLIAM
Pop, it doesn't have to be like this.
Why can't you understand? She's a person.
We are all part of the human race.
Black, white, red, yellow, it doesn't
matter, Pop.

BOB
It's those goddamn Jews
isn't it? They got to you.

WILLIAM
That does it, Pop. I gotta go.
Either you'll be there tonight
or you won't.

The phone clicks off. Bob slams down his receiver from his rotary phone.

Bob walks back to the table and takes a hefty swig from the bottle of Jack Daniels.

BOB
Sons a bitches.

Bob takes out another cigarette and lights it. He lets the smoke flow from his nostrils, like they are flaring.

He picks up the larger pieces from the broken glass and starts for the kitchen.

As he gets in, he starts to cough. The cough turns into a convulsion. The convulsion knocks the old man to his knees. He is starting a massive heart attack. He falls to the tiles of the kitchen, clutching his chest.

A light fills the room, bleeding all colors to white.

Bob stands, he is in white.

                    VOICE
                    Robert.

                    BOB
            Yes? Jesus, is that you?

                    JESUS
            Yes my son.

                    BOB
            I can't see you.

                    VOICE
            I am here.

Standing behind Bob is a tall black gentleman in brown robes and with long dread locks.

                    BOB
            It can't be. It can't be.

                    JESUS
            I am the shepherd, and you
                are the lamb.

BOB
(distraught)
No.

                                        IRIS OUT.

When I chose to shoot this, I decided not to play this on the phone but have it be in person. It felt better to be a character study of both the father and the son, as opposed to mostly a performance piece for the father alone playing to a telephone.

7

MINIVAN

Another of the shorts commissioned and not paid for, Minivan represents my pessimism towards the suburban lifestyles. Knowing too many people following this alleged American Dream into a mountain of debt and unhappiness with their 2.5 kids, generic cookie cutter homes, the one thing that represents that life choice is the Minivan. I wrote this based partially on a co-worker who hated his life and his family more than anything, yet stayed married; I fictionalized what his life would be when his 16 year old daughter would figure it all out.

EXT. INTERSTATE - DAY

It's a Monday and traffic is fairly light. This is out in the suburbs, so every two out of three automobiles is a mini van.

INT. BURGANDY MINIVAN - DAY

This is BRYAN McFEE's minivan, he is in his mid 30's, and a bit overweight, wearing a red polo shirt, and wearing a near permanent scowl.

MINIVAN

In the middle row are the twin girls, STACY and CHERYL, both are 8 years old and never ceasing to speak. Nex to them but in a booster seat is JOSH, a sparky, but clueless 5 year old boy in a family of girls. Lastly, in the very back of the minivan and sporting a nose ring, a navel ring, a tattoo on her shoulder, and jet black hair is the 15 year old daughter JACKIE.

STACY
Daddy are we there yet?

CHERYL
Yeah, daddy are we almost there yet?

BRYAN
(very annoyed)
No we aren't there yet, we just got
in the car, so we aren't there yet.
We're no where near there yet.

CHERYL
Daddy, do you know what
we made in school this week?

BRYAN
No pumpkin, what did you make?

CHERYL
I made a picture of a cow.

STACY
I made a picture of a volcano.

Not one to be outdone, but not quite with the conversation.

JOSH

I made a poo stink!

STACY
Ew! Dad he's gross. Are all boys
gross like him?

BRYAN
Ask your other sister.

JACKIE
I am not speaking to you.

BRYAN
I think someone's being a
grouch.

JACKIE
I think someone's neglecting
their paternal obligations.

BRYAN
(angry)
Watch it young lady.

JACKIE
(to the twins)
Let's play a game girls. Do you
want to play a game?

CHERYL
Yeah!

JACKIE
Let's take turns guessing why
daddy has been sleeping on the couch.
I think he smells bad and

that's why mommy doesn't
want him in the same room.

BRYAN
Enough of that.

CHERYL
I think he's lost too much hair
and momma doesn't want to keep
cleaning the shower drain.

BRYAN
Hey!

STACY
I think Momma doesn't want
daddy to wake her when he comes
home from working so late.

JOSH
I made a poo stink and Momma
says I am big.

BRYAN
That's fascinating Josh, really
it is.

JACKIE
Leave him alone. You should find
that interesting since you've barely
seen him since he was one.

BRYAN
That does it! Listen here, I have a very
important job. I provide you with the
money so you can go and permanently

damage your body.
(to the twins)
So you can afford to go to that private
school and draw pictures of a stupid cow.

The twins start to whimper.

BRYAN (CONT'D)
Oh no. No crying. No crying.

The girls start balling at full volume.

BRYAN (CONT'D)
(to Jackie)
Now do you see what you've done?

JACKIE
I didn't yell at them for no reason,
you did.

BRYAN
(to the twins)
Listen girls, girls are you listening
to me?
(they get down to sobs)
Daddy works very hard. Daddy has
to work extra hard and do things that the
other daddy's don't do. What I do
makes a difference.

JACKIE
You make it sound like you are a
fireman or a doctor. Selling soap to
hotels does NOT make a difference.

BRYAN

MINIVAN

It will make a difference when it comes
to review time. The harder I work, the
more money I stand to make, the more
likely I'll get promoted.

JACKIE
Maybe in your dreams. Do you really
think that being a kiss ass makes someone
higher up notice you? Do you think having
drinks with your supervisor three times a
week is the best way to show your
qualifications?

BRYAN
Watch your mouth. This is an important
part of networking.

JACKIE
Come on, dad. Haven't you ever noticed
the pattern yet? The people who work the
hardest never get ahead, they just get
stepped on when someone else moves up.

BRYAN
You sound so pessimistic.

JACKIE
Try realistic. Working all those extra
hours doen't make you more fulfilled,
you aren't more content. So what has it
gotten you? Nothing, but a bad back
sleeping on the couch while Mom spends
all of her time wondering why you
are so desperate not to come home.

Bryan is so flustered and fuming, that his eyes are red.

> BRYAN
> Jackie, you're worse than your
> mother. You are too young to
> under...

EXT. INTERSTATE - DAY
The mini van is moving faster than before and it runs straight into the back of the blue minivan right in front of it.

INT. BURGANDY MINIVAN - DAY

The air bags are blown and the twins are crying. Jackie is thrown from her seat and ont he floor of the car.
Bryan's face is covered with blood. He does not stir.

> JACKIE
> (starts to stir, hair in her face)
> Dad? Dad, are you all right?

Bryan does not move. Little Josh does not move either.

> JACKIE (CONT'D)
> Josh?
> (shaking his little immobile body)
> Josh, wake up! Oh no! Josh!

> FADE TO BLACK.

This is a dark, evil underbelly to suburbia and something I like to make fun of. Again, how comedic this can be is up to the director to play with.

RELATIONSHIP CARD

This 3rd in the trilogy of altered reality shorts, the writing exists because of being in a long term, co-habitating relationship. Combine that with an actual conversation with a co-worker who described the way her boyfriend "owed" her for various concessions, and her ability to track said concessions, and the idea for this was born.

Relationship Card took advantage of how visual FX can enhance the story and are not the expenditure they once were. Using 3D and 2D animation software that has lowered in price, as well as ingenuity with graphic design made this something that 10 years ago would have been nigh-impossible.

INT. KITCHEN - DAY

KATE, mid 20's, sips from her coffee as JIM, 30's, enters
            yawning.

                    JIM
            Morning.

                    KATE
            Morning. Hey, can you clean the

bathroom today? You said you'd do
that last weekend, remember?

                JIM
Oh, yeah. Look it's my day off. Can
I get to it later?

                KATE
That's what you said last week.

                JIM
I just want to ease into my day,
come on. Can't I wipe the toilet
down in a few hours?

                KATE
No! We agreed. I keep up my end of
the deal.

A long moment between them.

                JIM
Let's try the old "relationship
card".

Jim pulls out a card with the stripe on the back like a
credit card.

                JIM (CONT'D)
I'm so glad you put that big ol'
sexy brain of yours to work on
this. Once your patent on this
"relationship card" comes through,
we'll be rich.
Jim swipes the card through the machine on the kitchen counter.
It beeps and says "DECLINED" in the blue blocked letters.

RELATIONSHIP CARD

> JIM (CONT'D)
> Huh. It doesn't seem to be working.

It beeps a few more times.

> KATE
> Yes it does.

> JIM
> Then why isn't my transaction going
> through?

> KATE
> Because you're over drawn.

> JIM
> That's not possible.

> KATE
> Last night you used it to go to the
> game with your buddies and to get
> out of going to dinner with my
> parents.

Kate uses her hands and brings up a kind of virtual spreadsheet over the counter to show Jim his "account information".

> JIM
> Yeah, and that should balance out
> with me buying the groceries for
> the last month.

His account information is in RED and hers is in BLUE letters and graphics.

                    KATE
But I've made the mortgage payments
for the last three months.

                    JIM
What about me taking you out to
dinner on weekends?

                    KATE
Ah, that's not covered in the
"Terms of Service" contract you
signed when we agreed to use the
cards. You said that "date nights"
were still your little gift to me
and we agreed to exempt that from
the accounting.

A graphic of the lengthy terms of service with a zoom in on
his signature and date at the bottom get highlighted.

                    JIM
I got it. This doesn't account for
the fact that I got my friend to
fix the dry wall in the garage.

                    KATE
I paid for it.

                    JIM
Argh! Okay okay, let me see. What
about the HDTV?

                    KATE
What about it?

                    JIM

I bought that for us.

                    KATE
"Us"?

She stares him down.

                    JIM
          Okay, I bought that for me, but you
          still watch TV on it. That has to
          count for something.

                    KATE
          Fine, we can subtract few number of
          hours I spend watching TV versus
          the colossal amount of time wasted
          with reality shows that you do and
          we'll pro rate the ratio.

The graphic will be a pie chart with a small sliver representing Kate's TV watching.

Jim chews his fingernail.

                    JIM
          I paid the electric bill, the phone
          bill, and gas bill for June, July,
          and August and you never paid me
          back.

                    KATE
          And I paid your car payments for
          September and December.

The chart clearly shows a higher dollar amount for Kate.

                    JIM
          I've got it. One of the most
          important factors in my favor is
          not being accounted for.

Jim raises up a calendar with several (seventeen to be exact)
days highlighted.

                    KATE
          What's this?

                    JIM
          These are the dates we've had sex
          in the last month.

                    KATE
          And why is this supposed to go in
          YOUR plus column?

                    JIM
          Because I do it for you.

                    KATE
          Oh please.

                    JIM
          Add this to my plus column.

                    KATE
          I'm afraid I can't do that.

Kate overlays her own calendar (blue) over top of his (red -
making a purple calendar) with only 2 days highlighted.

                    JIM
          What's this?

                    KATE
          The only 2 times last month I've
          had an orgasm.

                                        CUT TO:

INT. BATHROOM - DAY

Jim is on his hands and knees scrubbing a toilet with a rag.

                                  FADE TO BLACK:

                              ____

REFRACTORY

*This drama represents a look at creating female roles that are
beyond the part of "blonde girl with breasts runs from killer
with a knife" that pervade the short films being made today.
Good roles for women are getting harder to find and this is
something for two women, one older, one younger, and has some
meat on the bones in performing.*

*The writing excersize lies in trying to make the dialogue mean
something different than it appears on the surface. Talking about
the weather is NOT talking about the weather. The contest of
wills has already begun.*

EXT. PSYCHIATRIC HOSPITAL - DAY

INT. HALLWAY - DAY

A MALE NURSE, 30's, wearing a white shirt and white pants
walks KIM, 20's, down a hallway. Kim wears the pink or off-
green patient uniform and has tattoos visible.

INT. DR. JO KIMBLE'S OFFICE - DAY

Dr. Jo has her back turned to Kim and stares out the window,
only half turning when the male nurse sets Kim in a chair,

almost pushing her down.

> JO
> I'm glad to see you're
> doing well.

> KIM
> I'm just swell.

Looking out the window.

> JO
> It's getting cold for this
> time of year.

> KIM
> Here, the wind always comes from
> the west heading east. In Europe, the
> wind goes from the East to West.

> JO
> Indeed. Now that we're here,
> how do you plan to proceed?

> KIM
> I plan to be a good girl. No
> more trouble from me.

> JO
> Time is a commodity. It's
> something that can be taken
> away or given as a gift.

> KIM

You don't say. Then I'm the
richest girl alive. I've got nothing
but time.

Dr. Jo writes on her page.

JO
Kim, this how this works. You have
to take your meds. You have to make
some progress, or you
and I will grow old together in
this place.

KIM
You've got quite a
headstart on me, Dr. Jo.

JO
Then tell me about your mother.

Silence.

JO (CONT'D)
Kim, I can help you. We have to begin
somewhere. You've already seen every
other doctor here.

KIM
Maybe I don't need help.

JO
That's not what your
mother says.

KIM

REFRACTORY

Is she qualified to make
a medical diagnosis?

JO
She's your mother.

KIM
So?

JO
Why did you do it? How often do
you get impulses?

Kim says nothing. Jo waits patiently.

JO
Your constant defiance will not serve
you well. Let's see how two more weeks in
solitary might straighten you out.

KIM
I just got out.

JO
You're not giving me any
choice, are you?

Kim jumps up on the desk like an animal and grabs a pen in her
hand. She starts to stab Dr. Jo in the throat

CUT TO:

Kim still sits staring at Dr. Jo, static.

KIM
I guess not.

JO
Nurse!

The male nurse re-enters the room.

JO (CONT'D)
Take her back to solitary room 3.

The male nurse grabs Kim's arm.

KIM
There's nothing wrong
with me.

JO
Then you should have talked.

KIM
I'll see you in two weeks.

Kim leaves the room shaking off the hand of the nurse. Jo sits at her desk and looks down at the paper.

INT. PADDED CELL - DAY

Kim sits with her arms around her legs, head down.

She looks up and the camera gets an EXTREME CLOSE UP of her eyes.

FADE TO BLACK:

10

The Knockout

This short film is actually a remake of the earlier Back Office story, fleshed out and intended to be more of a silent montage, a sound design film with details of how life is hard sometimes regardless of the efforts on puts in.

Meant to convey the systematic racism in the form of a metaphor for boxing, the Knockout was something that has almost been filmed several times. The storyboards by Brad Sherman really helped sell the transitions from the boxing ring into Darius' past. Each flashback takes you furth back in time. As his life is in peril, it flashes before his eyes with each hit and each moment in the match.

SHORT SCREENPLAYS

He who is not courageous enough to take risks will
accomplish nothing in life.
- Muhammad Ali

1 INT. - BOXING RING - NIGHT 1
The crowd reacts as DARIUS JACKSON, an African-
American, 21 year-old boxer, deftly deflects, then
dodges, a series of jabs and crosses thrown by the
other fighter, STORMY, a slightly larger bald boxer.
After DARIUS moves away from the punches both men
momentarily circle the ring, preparing to reengage.

DARIUS briefly takes in and assesses the moment.

                    ANNOUNCER ONE
          That was a nice evasion by Jackson
          there. He's doing a really good job
          of staying in this fight-a fight
          many would likely say he doesn't
          have a shot at winning. He's just
                         too-

                    ANNOUNCER TWO
            Well, he's giving the haters
            something to think about here
          tonight. Darius 'The Great' Jacksonthat's
            what he goes by right now-is
            not yet great, but he is a young
            tough fighter who's strong and
          resilient and, you know, he's got a
            good mind too. He figures things
            out in there. And all those traits
            add up to him being here now, still
             up on his feet, against a very,
                  very tough opponent.

                    ANNOUNCER ONE
            Yeah, one of the toughest.

MEDIUM shot of Darius' left gloved hand going for a
chest punch.

                                        CUT TO:

THE KNOCKOUT

2 INT. - GYM - DAY (TWO MONTHS AGO) 2

CU of Darius' left hand connecting to a punching
bag.

> TRAINER
> One of the toughest. That's what
> you got to be. Or else, what's the
> point?

DARIUS' face is glistening with sweat as he strains
to get out more push-ups. His boxing trainer,
TRAINER, squats on the floor next to him.

> TRAINER
> It's tough this out or go home. Go
> back to the projects. Go back on
> welfare. Go back to taking. And not
> making it happen. It ain't on
> anyone else. It's on you.

DARIUS nearly buckles from exhaustion. His arms
shake as he raises his torso.

TRAINER
> It's all on you. You got that? Are
> you going to raise yourself up?
> 'Cause I'm not going to do it for
> you.

DARIUS' chest lowers to the ground. His body,
trembling,begins to raise up again, slowly.

> TRAINER
> Are you going to raise yourself up?

> DARIUS
> (panting; through
> gritted teeth)
> I will.

> TRAINER
> Can't hear you, DJ.

                    DARIUS
          (a little more resolutely)
                    I will.

Against mounting resistance DARIUS finally lifts
himself back up. Thinking he's now done and before
he can collapse down to the floor-

                    TRAINER
          That's right. Now. Five more.

                    DARIUS
          (anger flashes across his
          face, then resolve)
                    I will!

3 INT. - BOXING RING - NIGHT 3

Darius has his gloves over his face, taking some
punches in stride. He starts to hit back and circle
his opponent.

                 ANNOUNCER ONE
          Jackson looks like he is holding
                 his own there.

                 ANNOUNCER TWO
          He looks a little over matched to
          me. Stormy is 9 and 1. He's taken
          down a lot faster opponents than
                     this.

DARIUS sits in his corner and a water bottle is
extended to him. He appears spaced out-he's
somewhere else-as he drinks from the straw. Hands
move over him, rubbing him, massaging the fatigue
from his body. He spits the water out off to the
side. The sound of the crowd grows louder as muffled
instructions are given to him. He stares ahead, his
breath heavy. Then, like a switch turning on, he
regains his focus.

His eyes narrow, he pops his mouthpiece back in and
he springs to his feet right before-DING! The bell

signals the start of the next round. DARIUS rushes forward, almost sprinting headlong back into the fight.

                                        CUT TO:

4 EXT. - STREET - NIGHT (A YEAR AGO) 4

DARIUS, his headphones on, jogs along the side of the street.

Every now and then he throws jabs into the air. He catches sight of flashing red and blue lights as he passes by a storefront window. A police cruiser speeds just past him and comes to an immediate stop ahead of him. This suddenness brings DARIUS' jog to an end.

Two white POLICE OFFICERS, one in his twenties and the other in his fifties, quickly exit the cruiser and approach DARIUS. The YOUNGER OFFICER has his hand on his holstered pistol as they both approach DARIUS.

                    DARIUS
                (pulling off his
                  headphones)
          Whoa. What's going on? What is
                    this?

                  OLDER OFFICER
          Take it easy son. We're responding
          to a call. What are you doing out
                    here?

                    DARIUS
              I'm running.
                YOUNGER OFFICER
                From what?

                    DARIUS
          From nothin'. I'm just out doing my
                  training.

                    YOUNGER OFFICER
            What's "training"? Training for
                         what?

                        DARIUS
              Why you stopping me?

                     OLDER OFFICER
             We got an APB on someone going
           around smashing side mirrors off of
               cars parked along the street.

DARIUS displays his hands to the OFFICERS showing
them he doesn't have anything to smash mirrors with
and that his hands are clean from any resultant
scrapes or cuts. The YOUNGER OFFICER steps to
DARIUS.

                     YOUNGER OFFICER
             I'm going to pat you down. You have
             any weapons on you or anything else
                   I should know about?

                      OLDER OFFICER
             Do you have any I.D. on you son?

DARIUS shakes his head and mouths "bullshit" as he's
pushed onto the hood of the squad car to receive the
patdown.

5 EXT. - STREET - NIGHT (A LITTLE LATER) 5
DARIUS is seated on the curb as the YOUNGER OFFICER
stands above him. DARIUS looks up, his eyes meet the
YOUNGER OFFICER'S and he senses no warmth, no
respect from those eyes. The OLDER OFFICER walks
back from the cruiser toward the men.

                      OLDER OFFICER
                   (speaking into his
                 shoulder-mounted radio)
                    Okay. Roger that.
                (to the YOUNGER OFFICER)
             They got the guy over on Fourth.
             This one here checks out; he's

                    clean.
                  (to DARIUS)
        Sorry to bother you. It happens.
            You can go on now.

DARIUS stands up from the curb and puts his
headphones back on.

                    DARIUS
         Free at last, free at last.

DARIUS shakes his head dismissively and goes back to
his run as both OFFICERS return to their cruiser and
drive off.

6 INT. - BOXING RING* - NIGHT 6

DARIUS is backed into a corner. A barrage of punches
from the OTHER FIGHTER keeps him pinned in. His
guard is up as he tries to slip out an opening off
to the side, but that just opens his body up to more
blows. He lowers an elbow to deflect the hits coming
into his body and that leaves enough space for a
devastating overhand hook to land right across
his face, snapping his head to the side.

7 INT. - GRANDMA'S APARTMENT - DAY (11 YEARS AGO) 7

GRANDMA'S slap lands right across 10 year-old
DARIUS' face.

                    GRANDMA
        I don't work this hard to take care
          of you-and your momma-for you to
         take what's not yours! I won't have
            a thief livin' under my roof.

GRANDMA, wearing her nurse's scrubs, stands over
little DARIUS. DARIUS's eyes fill up with tears as
he looks over at the kitchen table. An assortment of
mp3 players and Nintendo DSes lay spread out upon
it.

                    GRANDMA
        I know your momma didn't buy this
          for you. You goin' to be better
        than this, DJ. This kinda thingstealin-
               ain't for you. We're gonna
           find out where all this came from
              and you're gonna return it.

DARIUS nods, his grandmother's words take root.

8 INT. - BOXING RING - NIGHT 8

A furious series of punches strikes DARIUS and
launches him back into the ropes. He's covering
himself as he tries to slide away from the volley
being hurled upon him.

                  ANNOUNCER ONE
         This might be it! Darius Jackson is
           on the ropes fighting, he can't
         even bring his gloves up to defend
                    himself-

                  ANNOUNCER TWO
         He's doing everything he can just
         to withstand the damaging barrage
          being thrown at him right now!
         Darius Jackson can't possibly take
                   much more-

A single fist rockets upwards into DARIUS' jaw
snapping his head back and propelling his body
backwards.

                  ANNOUNCER ONE
          That's it! Jackson is going down!
             And his body falls ...

                  ANNOUNCER TWO
          That was a devastating blow. Once
          he got cornered ... He never had a
                    chance.

And his body falls ...

THE KNOCKOUT

                    ANNOUNCER TWO
                This one is over folks.
                He is down.He is done.

And his body falls. DARIUS hits the canvas, limbs
splayed out. Still conscious, he slowly rolls onto
his side. Eyes glassy as he stares off, back into
the distant past. He's listening to something.

9 INT. - DARIUS' BEDROOM - NIGHT (15 YEARS AGO) 9

Six year-old DARIUS is sitting up in his bed with
the side of his head pressed up against the wall. He
sits in darkness save for the streetlight entering
through his bedroom window.

He listens.

                  DARIUS' MOTHER (O.S.)
              You wanna just leave me? Just like
                    that? After all-

                      MAN (O.S.)
              I can't do this! I thought I could.
               But I'm not ready to be like a
               father to a boy who ain't mine.
                        (MORE)
              I'm not gonna be able to share you
              with...you got him. Ain't no room
                      left for me.

                    DARIUS' MOTHER
              You got no idea how hard it is on
              me! I didn't plan on having a son.
               I didn't want this. But I'm doing
              the best I can for him and me and I
              thought you knew that already. And
               I thought you could handle that.

                      MAN (O.S.)
              Well, I can't handle that. And this
                      is over.

A door slamming doesn't affect DARIUS as he sits and listens to the sound of his mother sobbing in the other room. DARIUS rubs his eyes.

10 INT. - BOXING RING - NIGHT 10
DARIUS lies motionless on his side as hands move above him, counting him out. His eyes are fixed, staring off. He breathes in slowly as muted voices announce the ending of the fight, and maybe the ending of his time as a fighter.

11 EXT. - PUBLIC PARK - DAY (FIFTEEN YEARS AGO) 11

DARIUS sits atop a slide cradling his legs as he rests his head on his knees. DARIUS' MOTHER stands a few feet away from him, exhorting him with her arms to come down.

                    DARIUS' MOTHER
              DJ. C'mon down.

DARIUS shakes his head 'no.'

                    DARIUS' MOTHER
              I know you heard some things last
              night. I'm sorry, baby. Truth is,
              you mean the world to me. When I
              was younger, I didn't know if I
              could be a mother. I didn't want-I
              wasn't ready to have a child. But
                    you know what?

DARIUS shakes his head 'no.'

                    DARIUS' MOTHER
              Then I had you. Then I had my own
              little boy and there's nothing more
              important or more loved by me than
                    you.

DARIUS' rigid composure wains slightly.

                    DARIUS' MOTHER
                (extending her hand up to
                          him)
              Darius. Baby. Come here to me.

After a moment DARIUS' countenance softens somewhat
and he slowly climbs down to take his mother's hand.
He looks down at her hand and then raises his eyes
up at her. Keeping his gaze up at her, he leans down
and kisses her hand.

12 INT. - BOXING RING - NIGHT 12

DARIUS breathes out slowly and is still.

                                        FADE OUT

Storyboards by Brad Sherman

Scene 1

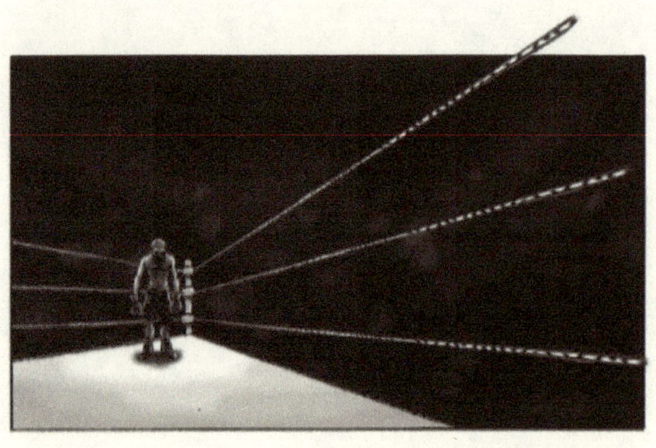

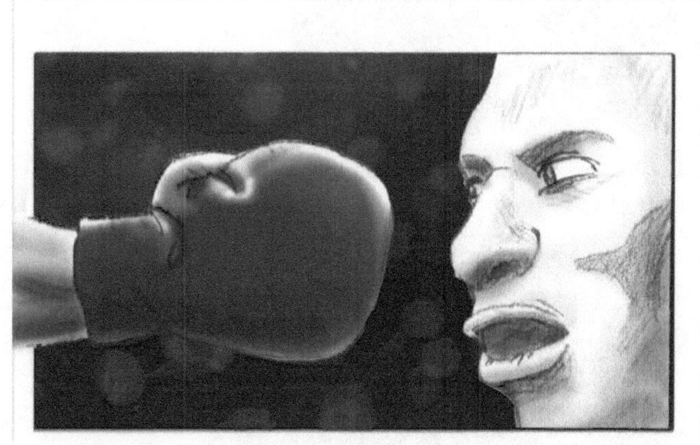

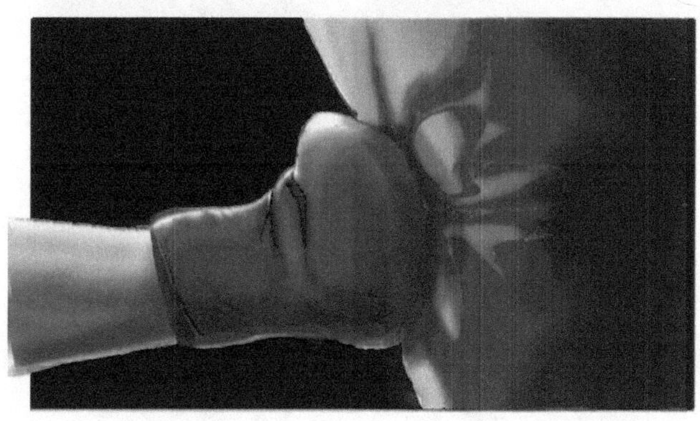

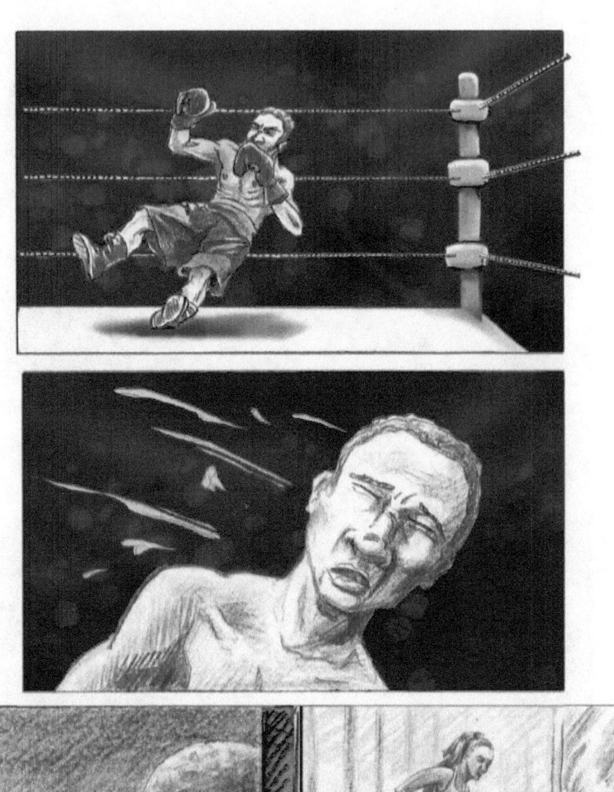

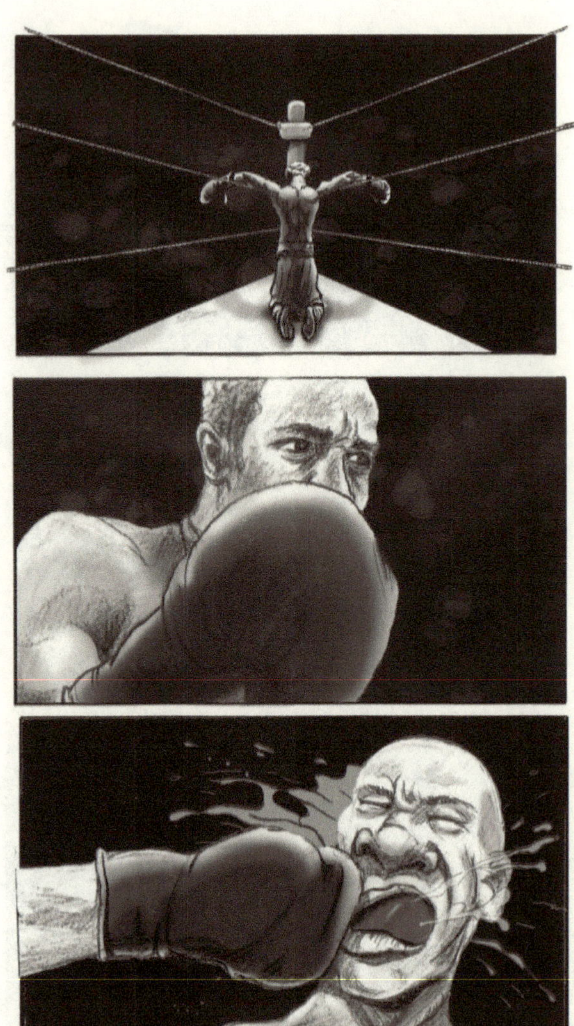

11

3:11AM

This script has no dialogue and is mean to be an entirely visual story. The ticking of the clock, the sequential aspect of reptitiveness is meant to symbolize how redundant life can be, how relationships fall into a consistent pattern.

The feeling of a metronome or how the music will beat on the moments, how time passes is meant to be shown by the shots being the same and in the end, one important thing will change. The decision to leave behind a life not worth living.

INT. BEDROOM - NIGHT

CU of alarm clock flashing 3:10AM as it turns
to 3:11AM

Overhead shot of a bed, on the left is a man
JOHN, spooning a woman on the right, SAMANTHA.
They are each wearing very light bed clothes.
CU of Samantha's face smiling. She reaches over
towards the clock.

                                        CUT TO:

INT. OFFICE - DAY
Her hand reaches for the cell phone. Samantha
sits at her desk. Her phone buzzes with a Text
message.

A graphic appears on screen showing the
contents of the text,as it says "So glad you
liked it. I love you, Pum'kin."

She smiles as she twirls a heart-shaped
necklace around her neck. Her boss enters the
frame standing, we do not see his face, as
Samantha turns back to her desk and work.

The camera dollies left

                                       WIPE TO:

INT. KITCHEN TABLE - AFTERNOON

Camera dollies into Samantha placing plates of
food on the table for John. He kisses her on
the cheek and she smiles.

INT. BEDROOM - NIGHT

CU of alarm clock flashing 3:10AM as it turns
to 3:11AM

3:11AM

Overhead shot of a bed, on the left is a man JOHN, spooning a woman on the right, SAMANTHA.

Their night clothes are a little different, slightly warmer clothes.

CU of Samantha's face smiling less than before.

She plays with the necklace in her fingers. She reaches over towards the clock.

CUT TO:

INT. OFFICE - DAY

Samantha, still a slight smile, toys with the necklace in her fingers, and puts it down when her phone vibrates again.

The text appears as a box again on screen, "What are we having for dinner tonight, Pum'kin??"

She rolls her eyes a little and her BOSS enters the frame from right, he's only seen from the waist down, she starts to spin back to her computer and work.

WIPE TO:

INT. KITCHEN TABLE - AFTERNOON

Samantha and John are eating at the table, not talking.

INT. BEDROOM - NIGHT

CU of alarm clock flashing 3:10AM as it turns to 3:11AM

149

Overhead shot of a bed, on the left is JOHN, spooning Samantha on the right.

Their night clothes are a little different, warmer clothes.

CU of Samantha's face, entirely neutral. She turns her head.

She reaches over towards the clock.

                                    CUT TO:

INT. OFFICE - DAY

Again, Samantha's face entirely neutral. Her phone starts to buzz. She lets it go longer than before.

Frustrated, she looks at the text, which appears on screen.

"Can you pick up some toothpaste on your way home, Pum'kin?"

                                    WIPE TO:

INT. KITCHEN TABLE - AFTERNOON

Samantha and John are clearly yelling at each other. Her arms are folded and John paces nearby, hand on his brow.

INT. BEDROOM - NIGHT

CU of alarm clock flashing 3:10AM as it turns to 3:11AM

Overhead shot of a bed, on the left is JOHN, back to back with Samantha. When he rolls over and puts his arm around her.

CU of Samantha's face as his arm goes around her. She does not like it.

INT. OFFICE - DAY

Samantha in a warmer sweater at her desk, the phone vibrates.

She picks it up and looks at the text message, appears on screen.

"Have to work late tonight."

WIPE TO:

INT. KITCHEN TABLE - AFTERNOON

Samantha at the table with a plate in front of her alone.

INT. BEDROOM - NIGHT

CU of alarm clock flashing 3:10AM as it turns to 3:11AM

OVERHEAD shot of John alone in the bed.

Reverse shot to the door, where Samantha is fully dressed, in a heavy coat with a suitcase at her side. She turns off the hall light.

FADE TO BLACK

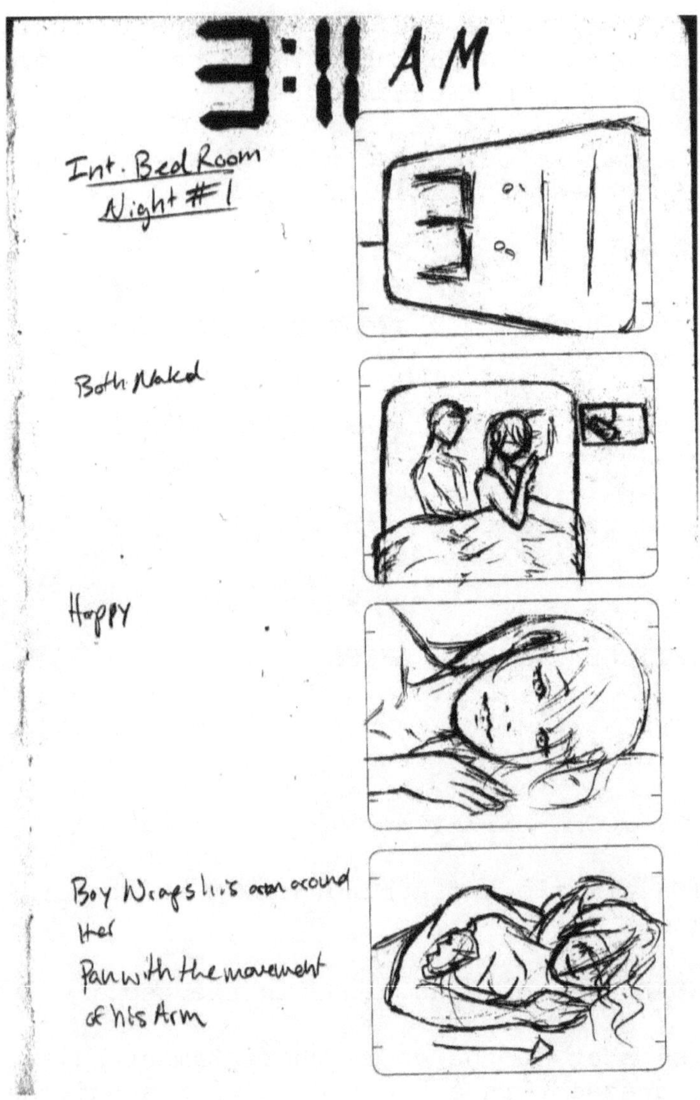
3:11 AM
Int. Bed Room
Night #1
Both Naked
Happy
Boy Wraps his arm around
Her
Pan with the movement
of his Arm

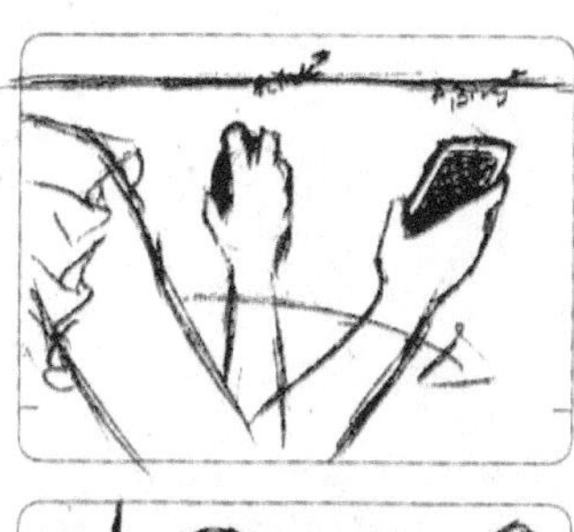

Int. Office Day #1

Picks up phone

Swings Chair around to read text
Playing with necklace

Boss comes in
looks up with Apology

Right to Left Dolly
Boss walks out of frame
Back to Doing Work

Int. Kitchen

Afternoon #1

Dolly Right to left
leans over and Kisses her
as she puts food on the
table

Int. BedRoom

Night #2

. Already Spooning
Lace Nighty
No Shirt

playing with necklace

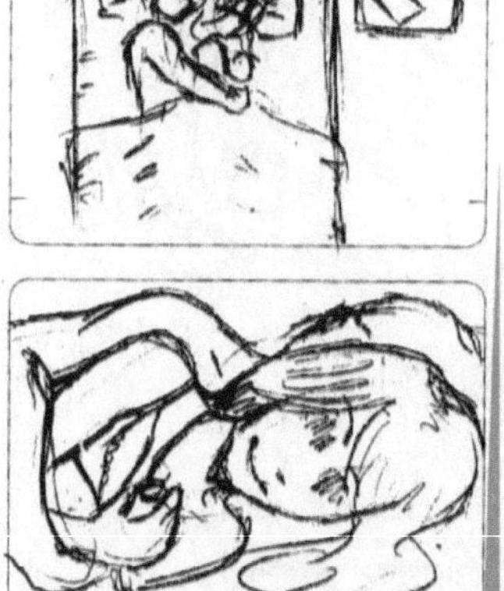

Int. Office Day #2

Short Sleve
(Dark Royal Rich color)

Less Defiant to Boss
Boss wipes the
Screen

Int Kitchen Afternoon #2
Eating Diner Not
Talking

Int. Bedroom Night #3

Girl - Tank top
Boy - T-shirt

Neutral Face

Int Office Day #3

Annoyed

Boss doesn't even stop

Long sleeve (light grey tone)
Slacks

Dolly Right to left

Int. Kitchen Afternoon #3
Girl - Jeans, light long sleeve
Boy - Khaki, Bottandown
Fighting !!!

Dolly Right to Left
Int. BedRoom Night #4

Back to Back
Both - Thicker PJs

Boy tries to put arm
around her
Rolls over

Girl Repulsed
Shove

Int Office Day #4
Doesn't even look at text
Boss Walks right by
Sweater - Scarf
Dark Grey / Black

Dolly Right to Left

Int. Kitchen Afternoon #4

Hoodie
Jeans

Guy isn't there
Drinking Wine Alone

Int. Bed Room
Night #5

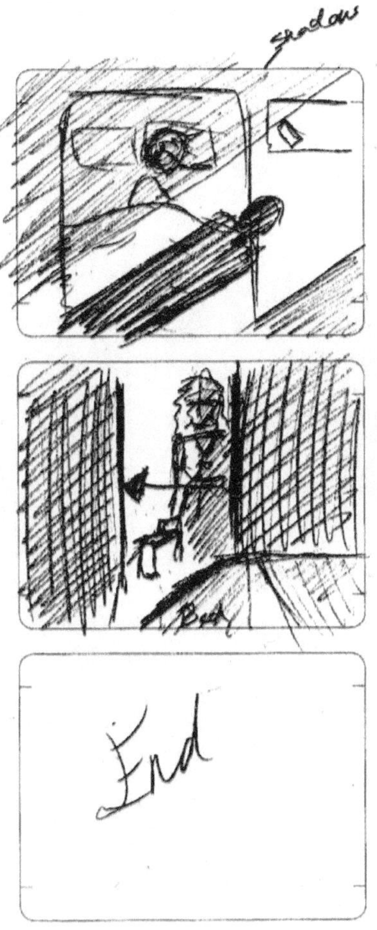

Alone in Bed
Her Shadow Crossing
H.gn

Half in shadow leaving
with sodcase

12

FIRST BORN

Inspired by Joss Whedon and his sardonic wit, this short film is meant to be funny and played in something of a sitcom style, almost as if these characters live in a different internal world with it's own rhythm.

EXT. SUBURBAN HOUSE - NIGHT

Truck left to right on a ranch house, light in the bedroom turn off.

INT. CHILD BEDROOM - NIGHT

SARAH, late 20's/early 30's flips off a light switch, looking into a crib where BABY DAVID, infant is lying.

                    SARAH
          Goodnight sweetheart.

Dolly out from the crib past a baby monitor.

INT. KITCHEN - NIGHT
iPhone phone rings, Sarah answers.

                    SARAH
          Hi mom. I just put David down. No,
                  I'm fine.

Sarah puts dishes away from sink. She plays with an
odd necklace around her neck.

CU on the Fridge, a photo of Sarah in a hospital
holding a baby with her husband, then condolence
cards stuck on by magnets.

                    SARAH (CONT'D)
          Mom, of course I'm wearing it. No,
          really. I'll manage. Okay? I've got
                  to go.

Sarah puts the iPhone down and just exhales.

EXT. SUBURBAN HOUSE - NIGHT

Dolly in towards the house.

INT. CHILD BEDROOM - NIGHT

An orange glow starts to emit near the crib.

INT. KITCHEN - NIGHT

CU of the baby monitor as a whooshing sound starts
and the baby starts to cry.

Sarah looks over and runs down the hall.

INT. CHILD BEDROOM - NIGHT

Sarah runs in as a giant orange ball of fire grows
and out steps an enormous, RED DEMON with horns
wearing a toga. Each foot lands with a thud.

Sarah's eyes go wide as the orange ball collapses
into itself.

A long beat as Sarah looks at the demon.

                    TODD
                    Hi.

Sarah just stares

                    TODD (CONT'D)
                  I'm Todd.

FIRST BORN

                    SARAH
                 Uh, what?

                    TODD
      My name is Todd. I'm here for your
        first born. Is this the little
                   fella?

Todd moves towards the crib. Sarah moves to block
him.

                    SARAH
              Don't touch him!

                    TODD
      Hey relax. I'm just doing my job.

                    SARAH
                 What job?

                    TODD
            You agreed to this!

                    SARAH
        I've never made a deal with the
                   devil.

She twirls the necklace around her neck.

                SARAH (CONT'D)
              Is this about...

                    TODD
      That? The devil? No. Apple? Yes.

                    SARAH
         What are you talking about?

                    TODD
          You have an iPhone right?

                    SARAH
                   Yeah.
          Sarah pulls out her phone.

                    TODD
        You agreed to the end user license
              agreement, right?

Todd creates a terms of service agreement in flaming
letters.

                    TODD (CONT'D)
          Right here in the thirty seventh
          paragraph, it clearly states that
          if you want to use the extended
          applications that you agree to give
          up your first born child, so come
                  on. Let me just...

He moves towards the crib, and Sarah stands her
ground.

                      SARAH
          I am not letting you take my son to
          some hell dimension for the rest of
                    his life!

                      TODD
            Rest of his life? We're not
          monsters. It's just for a couple
          years. He's got those tiny digits.
          Really helpful for making iPhones.
          So come on, let's get this show on
                    the road.

                      SARAH
          Do you really work for Apple?

                      TODD
          No, I'm a subcontractor working for
          the law firm that represents Apple.
          Lawyers, am I right? I'm on a
                  schedule, so...

                      SARAH
          I just signed up with Verizon. I'll
          be paying on this for at least four
          years. Isn't there anything we can
                      do?

                      TODD
          Sure, you can give up your iPhone.

Sarah looks to her phone, looks back to Todd, looks
back to her phone, and looks back to Todd.

                      SARAH
          Isn't there anything like a Charlie
          Daniels provision or something?

                      TODD
          Well, you can always challenge me.
          I have to warn you though, I
          studied violin with a poor soul who
          studied at Julliard. DO you really
          think you can out fiddle me?

FIRST BORN

                    SARAH
          No. Any other options other than
                    music?

                    TODD
          There is another challenge. A far
          more ancient and provocative
          contest that has claimed more souls
          than the wars of Karesh and the
          battle of tears unnumbered.

                                        CUT TO:

INT. LIVING ROOM - NIGHT

OVERHEAD shot of a game of Scrabble.

Todd and Sarah are sitting on a couch and love seat
over a coffee table, set with candles, looking like
a ceremony.

                    TODD
          With the "Q" on the triple score,
          that gets me 24 points. How do you
          like them apples?

                    SARAH
          You don't look like a guy would use
          a work like quixotic.

Sarah lays out the word "CUNT" on the board.

                    TODD
          Classy.

                    SARAH
          When I play, I play to win.
Time passes. Todd is adding up the score.

                    TODD
          So I've got 231 and you
          have....197. Sorry.

                    SARAH
          Okay, double or nothing.

                    TODD
          What else are you offering me? I've
          got your son for a few years and
          your soul for all eternity.

                    SARAH
          What about this?

She grabs a few CD's from her shelf.
                    TODD
          John Mayer? Just how evil do you

                        think I am?
Todd shrugs.

                    TODD (CONT'D)
          Fine. Let's do one more challenge.

                                        CUT TO:

INT. KITCHEN - LATER

Sarah and Todd are standing side by side throwing
ping pong balls into red cups.

Todd is nailing his shots. Sarah gets frustrated.

                    SARAH
               Damn it!

                    TODD
          I pledged Sigma Alpha Epsilon
               in college.

INT. LIVING ROOM - LATER

Sarah and Todd are sitting on the floor with a deck
of cards out, each with some cards in their hands

                    TODD
               So?

Sarah's eyes squint. Long beat before

                    SARAH
               Go fish.

After some more playing, Todd sweeps up the cards.
Sarah takes off her necklace and tosses it at Todd.

INT. LIVING ROOM - LATER

Todd is holding his John Mayer CD's, a book, a
picture, and more.

                    TODD
          All right, so now I have your
          little boys digits, John Mayer
          CD's, some rather curious wall art,
          a family recipe that I am being
          assured is not available anywhere
          else, and a talisman that will make
          my roommate giggle. Time we mosey
          on out of here and get this show on
               the road.

                    SARAH
          Wait... Before we go, can I offer
          you something before we go?

Sarah goes to a shelf and starts to open a basket.

                    TODD
          Listen, I've really got to...

Sarah pulls out a bag of weed.

                    TODD (CONT'D)
          Okay, I can stay for a little bit.

                                        CUT TO:

INT. LIVING ROOM - LATER

Todd takes a big hit from a bong.

                    TODD
          No. The fourth dimension isn't
          time. That's a common
          misconception.

Sarah takes a hit.

                    SARAH
          What is it then?

                    TODD
          Ever hear of the tesseract? There's
          a whole other physical dimension,
          several actually. There's a
          dimension where trees are sentient
          and they get really pissed at wood
          houses.

                                        CUT TO:

INT. LIVING ROOM - LATER

Todd stands up, a little dizzy.

                    TODD
          Seriously, this has been fun and
          all, but we've got to go. Wait,
          what was I here for again?

                    SARAH
          I don't, uh....

                    TODD
          Wait, was that your plan? Get me so
          high I forget what I'm here for?
          Listen lady, I hang out with Bob
          Marley's ghost, and this was pretty
          good stuff, but come on.

                    SARAH
                (exasperated)
        Please. What else can I do? There
        has to be some kind of loop hole,
        some way for me to save my son. My
        husband just died. I just need some
                 kind of break.

Todd takes a deep breath.

                    TODD
        Okay, I normally don't do this, and
        this is worse than going to hell
        for a few years, but there is one
                other option.

                    SARAH
                I'll take it.

                    TODD
        You really need to think about
        this. Very few people take this
        option because its considered the
               worst possibility.

                    SARAH
           I have to. For my son.
        Todd takes a deep breath.

                    TODD
                 Okay.

Todd opens a fire portal with his fist raised.

                                        CUT TO:

INT. APPLE STORE - DAY

Sarah is wearing a blue polo shit with the apple
logo on it and she stands before a wall with the
apple logo on it.

                    SARAH
        Welcome to the genius bar, my name
           is Sarah can I help you?
              (mutters to herself)
             What have I done?

                                    FADE TO BLACK

INTERVIEW COLLECTION

WIKIPEDIA INTERVIEW 2008

Wikinews held an exclusive interview with American author and filmmaker Peter John Ross. The head of Sonnyboo Productions, an independent film studio based in Columbus, Ohio, he has made numerous short films as well as co-directed a feature, the World War II B-movie Horrors of War.

He has also written a book on filmmaking, Tales from the Front Line of Indie Filmmaking. He says that it "combines helpful articles for beginning filmmakers with narrative tales based on my experiences raising money for features and the crazy personalities that invade the world of microbudget filmmaking."

When asked why he makes movies, Ross replied, "There is no greater thrill than sitting in a room full of strangers watching the stories unfold with flickering pictures and sound. I live for the moments when I can sit there and watch the movies with people I don't know and really feel how they react to what I wrote or directed or edited."

You've made several short films and co-directed a feature, Horrors of War. Tell us about them.

Mr. Ross: I could not afford film school, so I set out to make my own movies and teach myself filmmaking. Each short I made for the Internet had a specific goal in mind to teach myself some new technique or challenge myself in a new way. To me it was all about "graduating" to making a feature film. After 5 years of making shorts online, most in digital, but some in actual film as well, I felt ready to tackle a feature film. Working with many of the people I had been for years, we set out to make an ambitious World War II Nazi Zombie Werewolf movie. Horrors of War is an homage to the "B" movie tradition, in that grindhouse style. We used the Internet to promote and market the film by putting out MAKING OF segments and helpful filmmaker tips.

Horrors of War was shot entirely in Ohio, which doubled for France and Germany, on a shoestring budget. How did you manage this?

Mr. Ross: We used World War II re-enactors in the film as featured extras; they in turn brought tanks, armoured cars, authentic weapons and uniforms, and more. We shot a D-Day re-enactment on Lake Erie with 300 extras and even a real P-51 Mustang buzzing overhead. This made our movie look a whole lot bigger and better. When I was on a train trip in 1997 going from Paris to Heidelberg, I noticed that the hills, grass, and trees all reminded me of Ohio. For our film, we chose the pine tree locations to represent Germany, as they are similar to the Ardens, and other parts of the state to represent France.

Why do you make movies? What inspires you to do this?

Mr. Ross: There is no greater thrill than sitting in a room full of strangers watching the stories unfold with flickering pictures and sound. I live for the moments when I can sit there and watch the movies with people I don't know and really feel how they react to what I wrote or directed or edited. I love to tell stories and moviemaking is one of the most unique and immersive ways to tell a story. The payoff is always when you get to show your movies, especially in a theatrical setting.

Do you have any advice for the amateur filmmakers reading this?

Mr. Ross: Start small, then work your way up. Help on other people's productions and get an idea of what it really takes to make a movie, then start making small movies with a cheap camcorder and really get good at the art of telling stories with a camera before investing a lot of money into gear. It's the artist, not the brush that counts. Everyone thinks because they watch a lot of movies or TV that somehow qualifies them to make a good movie. No one thinks because they listen to a lot of music, they can buy a guitar and suddenly play like Jimi Hendrix. Why should movies be any different? Much like music, filmmaking requires practice to get good at it. Making short movies for the Internet is great practice. Go for it.

CRACKLE INTERVIEW 2007

Sonnyboo, nee Peter John Ross, has 56 clips on Crackle. 56! Somehow, this wildly efficient and enthusiastic filmmaker found time to answer our questions. If he sounds distracted, it's possible that he was directing a movie at the same time as the interview.

Crackle: Tell us about yourself. How did you get into filmmaking? Was this a lifelong goal?

PJR: I originally wanted to be a composer for films. When I finally got the chance to be on a soundtrack, I was so disappointed with the movie, I said to myself "I can do better". At the time I started making movies, I was working as a broker full time. I was fired for making movies on the premises (the office is featured in many of my videos on Crackle).

I was writing screenplays but never tried to make anything until I met Richard Linklater in 2000. We talked after a lecture and he asked me why I hadn't made a movie yet. I told him I wanted to shoot on film but didn't have the money. He asked me if I considered digital video. I scoffed and he got angry and asked me what was more important, owning film stock or telling a story. Within two weeks I had bought a digital camera. I have never been this poor and I have never been this happy in all my life.

Crackle: You've done TV spots as well. Do you find directing ads to be rewarding, or is it just a way to pay the bills and buff the resume?

PJR: TV spots are my day job. There are far worse ways

to make a living and it's rewarding in its own way. I still try to challenge myself artistically in commercial work. Short films are more manageable for control freaks. As Joss Whedon said, I'm not a control freak; I'm more of a control enthusiast.

Crackle: Your "How to Deal With Telemarketers" clip is a big hit in our office, although the sobbing telemarketer at the end whets our appetite for something totally different in tone. Any plans for a heartfelt drama about the miserable life of a lonely call-girl, so to speak?

PJR: We have an alternate ending shot where the telemarketing girl puts a gun in her mouth and we see blood splatter on an inspirational poster. In the end, I chose to go lighter, albeit not much lighter. I have no sympathy for telemarketers. Alicia Ritchey, the actress, actually worked as a telemarketer.

Crackle: Your "Film School Graduate" is a Kubrick-obsessed plumber with an ass crack not even a mother could love. Is this just a minute-long character study, or reflective of your general opinion about film school and the people it produces?

PJR: Actually, my opinion is very much that if you can afford film school – GO TO FILM SCHOOL. It's too valuable not to, but if you can't afford it, don't let that stop you either. I didn't go to film school. Film School Graduate pokes fun at anyone whose career does not involve their [college] major.

Crackle: Can you talk a little bit about the being an independent filmmaker in a city not known for its film?

PJR: Columbus, Ohio or "Cowtown" as it's known in many circles, has a little film scene. The digital video revolution has changed the playing field entirely. Small production companies (or individuals pretending to be production companies like myself/Sonnyboo Productions) can produce high quality content with little to no resources. The sky is the limit as far as what you can do with your imagination and a camera.

In Columbus, I have an easier time getting mentioned in national magazines than I do in the local ARTS papers. The reason Columbus is not known as a film town is because no one in Columbus wants to support film FROM Columbus. In January, the local moguls are giving Spike Lee $50,000 and Columbus filmmakers nothing. Why does Spike Lee need $50,000? I don't think he's even flown over Columbus, Ohio before.

The positive side to being a filmmaker in Columbus is that I don't have to pay for locations and there aren't too many people doing this. There's still some magic to making movies here as opposed to burned out, Hollywood cynicism and more apathy. I can remain somewhat pure in my motivations; although anytime I use someone else's money to make a movie I try to be as responsible as possible.

PULP MOVIES INTERVIEW 2005

Peter John Ross Founded in 1999, Sonnyboo short films have played on 3 continents and at over 50 film festivals world wide. Projects directed by Peter John Ross have appeared on Tech TV, National Lampoon Networks, Movieola the short film channel, The "U" Network, and Vegas Indies TV. Sonnyboo films have been noted in such publications as RES Magazine, Ain't It Cool News, Camcorder & Computer Video magazine, Film & Video Magazine, LA Weekly, Film Threat, the Village Voice, & Internet Video Magazine.

Sonnyboo founder and award winning filmmaker, Peter John Ross talks to Dale Pierce about the joys and hazards of independent filmmaking.

Dale: Where are you and your company located?

Peter: I am Peter John Ross with Sonnyboo.com and we are located in Columbus Ohio USA

Dale What are some of the productions you have done yourself?

I've done over 30 short films, and they are on my site and about 2 dozen additional short film/entertainment sites too. I wanted to learn how to make movies, so I just started making movies with a DV camcorder & a capture card on my PC. Now I'm shooting mostly on film, and moving into the new High Def arena.

You have dealt in shorts pretty much? Have you also done feature films?

So far I have written & directed all short films, worked on several feature length movies for other people.

Any future plans?

I am working on my own first feature film Horrors of War to shoot in May-July this summer. It's a World War II horror film, being shot on film.

You have also organized some film festivals, correct?

Yes, I have organized 15 different local/regional film festivals & screenings in Central Ohio. Thanks to this new form of "Microcinema", the new buzz word for sub-$10,000 moviemaking, mostly digital, the landscape has changed. Thanks to digital projectors, the wall of a coffee house becomes an exhibit of locally made movies, or landing on the real big screens at the local Cineplex.

The most recent festival was April 9th, 2005 Look at my Shorts Film Festival where we screened 13 short films to 350+ people.

Did you study film anywhere in school or simply enter the world and learn as your progress continued?

A little bit of both. I went to Bowling Green State University to study music, and after one whole semester of bureaucracy, I declared Liberal Arts major, and started taking classes like "Philosophy of Film", and a literature class where you read a novel, watch a movie, then watch a remake & write critiques of all three.

I have never taken a film or video production course.

All that & the techinicals I learned by just getting a computer, a camcorder & then I simply started making movies (and mistakes, from which I learned from). See Advice below.

What is your favourite film genre?

Good Movies. I don't care if it's a chick flick, action movie, sci fi, or whatever, as long as it's good.

What advice would you give people wanting to get involved with independent cinema?

Start small & work your way up/ No one ever goes into a guitar store, buys a Fender Strat, then expects to play like Hendrix, so why is it every yahoo with a camcorder & a computer thinks they are Robert Rodrieguz? Like all arts, no one can do it the first time & make a great piece of art. You have to practice to get good, like anything else from athletics to music to painting.

For all the beginners and soon to be filmmakers, my advice is to start with simple things like writing, then shooting, then editing a simple scene. Set attainable goals, then meet them and progress and challenge yourself. Learn how to do tell a story with moving pictures & sound. It is possible to jump right in & make a feature length movie, but the chances that it the first things you shoot are as good as the last things, given all that will be learned in that process, it's unlikely you'll have a balanced movie.

There's also something to be said about accomplishing something from these little shoots and getting in the habit of finishing. One of the most common cliché's in the indie film & microcinema world is starting projects & not finishing them. It's a waste of everyone's time. Making reasonable expectations yield more likely completion. This is just my opinion.

Aside from your Midwestern home base do you enter your projects overseas or make the indy film convention circuit?

My movies have played at film festivals all over the world including France, England, Ireland, Japan, China, Australia, Germany, Spain, and Canada. Like I stated earlier, there are festivals of every size cropping up in every city in the world. Some are free, some are only $5 to enter, and others are the $25-50 range. To me, all I care about it getting my movies seen. I make movies so that I can share a story with others. There is nothing like sitting in a dark room with a bunch of strangers watching a story unfold.

Today (April 11th, 2005), several of my movies are playing at the Shakespearean Globe Theatre in London UK, they are also streaming the event with bands & movies in an online simulcast.

Where could interested people get in touch with you or order your projects?

Sonnyboo.com, I have a message board where I answer questions, as well as the usual contact page. I'm also selling a DVD of most of my movies for $7.99

Any closing comments?

Thanks to the new technology of firewire, digital video, and non linear editing – it means anyone direct. Not everyone can direct well. Learn as you go & keep making movies.

MOVIES ONLINE INTERVIEW 2006

Writer/director/producer Peter John Ross recently took time out of his busy schedule to chat with us about life, favorite movies, and his upcoming film "Horrors of War"... and I gotta say he's one cool and hardworking guy.

MoviesOnline: What are some of your favorite films, horror and otherwise?

Peter John Ross: My favorite films are (in no particular order) Blade Runner, Brotherhood of the Wolf, Fellowship of the Rings, Star Wars (1977), A Clockwork Orange, and Porky's.

MO: Did anything specific lead you into a career as a filmmaker?

PJR: I was working as a broker for a large bank and after meeting Richard Linklater (Dazed & Confused, A Scanner Darkly), we had a long talk and I was very inspired. Shortly after, I had made a few short films, lost my brokerage job (fired for making movies about office llife on the premises). I've been full time filmmaker ever since. I've never been this poor or this happy in my life.

MO: How important is traditional schooling, do you think,

for an ambitious filmmaker?

PJR: If you can afford it, go to film school. There are more important relationships and networking available to film school students aside from great equipment & an environment conducive to making movies.

BUT, don't let $ stop you. For a few hundred $ you can teach yourself everything you need to know. I never went to film school and I got a $60,000 film school education for $1.50 in late fees at the public library (I have to quote my sources - that was James Cameron in 1991 on Howard Stern, (later) ripped off by Matt & Ben for GOOD WILL HUNTING 1997).

Anyone can get a camcorder and a home PC and learn to make movies. It's a dangerous thing because anyone CAN make films, but not everyone can make them WELL. Like any other art form, practice makes perfect. No one buys a guitar at a music store then expects to play like Hendrix right out of the box, so why does every yahoo with a camcorder think they'll be Kubrick on their first movie? They think because they watch a lot of movies they're qualified to make one, but that's not different than being someone who listens to a lot of classical music expects to write a symphony with no experience. Learn the craft, pratice first.

Ambition is the key. Hold on to that energy & keep trucking.

MO: Horrors of War is set during WWII. How much research into military history did you have to do for this film?

PJR: We had WWII re-enactors and several other experts consulting on the film. We did do research and made sure the names of places were correct and dates. The entire concept was based on the fact that Hitler did try several experiments on prisoners and soldiers, we just embellished and took it into a realm where it made a good horror story. Other changes from fact came from economic constraints being an independent, we couldn't always have the exact correct uniforms or props, but it's probably 85-90% accurate.

MO: The premise of the film is that Hitler has unleashed a secret weapon in order to fight off the advancing allied soldiers. Are the infected soldiers... zombies?

PJR: Heh, I won't say exactly what they are. There are two major types of experiments, one is lycan in nature, and the others are.. I'll let that one go for now.

MO: Are there any specific films or directors who have inspired your work?

PJR: George Lucas when I was 5 years old opened my mind to imagination. Not long after Spielberg really had a major influence. Nowaways, I love Stanley Kubrick for his movies, but seeing the documentaries on how he acted to cast & crew was pretty brutal, and by contrast I'm very moved by the lovefest that is the making of LORD OF THE RINGS and KING KONG with Peter Jackson. I think the teamwork & care shows in the work.

I like the collaborative process a lot. Horrors of War is co-directed & co-written by John Whitney, co-written and produced by Phil Garrett, produced by Sean Reid. We don't want to have ego-central on our movies. We directed the two halves of the movie separately, but edited it together as one whole together.

MO: Do you think war is a necessary path to peace?

PJR: Rarely, but yes. I think Hitler was the last clear "bad guy" in human history. That's why WWII stories appeal to me. It's a clear good guy/bad guy scenario and we, as viewers don't get that very much any more.

A WWIII vet made it clear as to how that was different than now. We were attacked, and there was a clear enemy. It's not like today where we're trying to declare war on abstract concepts. A "war on terror"? Give me a break, why don't we declare a "war on bad feelings" too.

MO: Horrors of War seems to have quite a bit of computer animation as well as traditional special effects and make up, which do you prefer?

PJR: We used CGI to enhance the scope of a few shots and to do the planes. Aside from that, it's sparingly used. I love CGI, but I think in camera is always better. I'm not some film purist that will not use something because it isn't natural. I'm all about what works best & what we can afford.

The CGI planes were done by Don Drennan, and the onset makeup was created by Tom Savini make up school graduate Shawn Collins.

MO: Is there any stock footage of battles in the film?

PJR: There is NO STOCK FOOTAGE OF ANY KIND used in the film. For anything "aged", we shot a D-Day re-enactment in September 2004 on Super 8 black & white film and it came out exactly like old newsreel and combat footage. There is nothing in this film that wasn't created specifically for Horrors of War.

MO: How difficult was it to stage the battle scenes?

PJR: Very. Safety is a big concern. The re-enactors are very experienced with blank firing and explosions, but we add the factor of a film crew and cast, and we all have to be very sensitive and paranoid about not getting anyone hurt.

Special FX (meaning on set practical FX) coordinator Rick Fike was very good about keep everyone alert and safe.

Choreography involving tanks, trucks, and a canon were of particular fun because it was a lot of extras and explosions and guns. A really good AD (Assistant Director) team on radios kept everything running smooth and organized.

MO: Why did you decide to use WWII as a setting for the film, and do you touch on the Holocaust?

PJR: We do not broach the topic of the holocaust at all. I think any kind of "horror movie" elements can't really touch the atrocity of what really went on.

They say the best fiction represents a metaphor for something real. Germans and Nazis as demons works, but

I can't really find anything worse than what they really did then to the Jews, artists, gays, and others sent to concentration camps.

MO: What sort of audience is this film geared to?

PJR: Horrors of War is specifically a hybrid Horror/Action/Sci Fi film. It's for the type of audience who digs horror and want to see something a little different, a "crossover" kind of film if you will.

MO: When will we be able to see Horrors of War?

PJR: Sometime in 2006 Horrors of War will be released in the U.S. and worldwide on DVD. We're also in talks to make it on TV. My hope is to get it on the SCI FI CHANNEL, but we'll have to see. We have to compete with "Mansquito" for air time.

ABOUT PETER JOHN ROSS – Ross has been nominated  for four regional Emmy's for his work on the television program Framelines, specifically for the educational and interactive projects that became Cinestudy. Ross has also directed feature films and shorts that have garnered him over 50 awards at festivals and online. He has also published several books on filmmaking.

www.sonnyboo.com

ABOUT CINESTUDY - Cinestudy originated as the Emmy 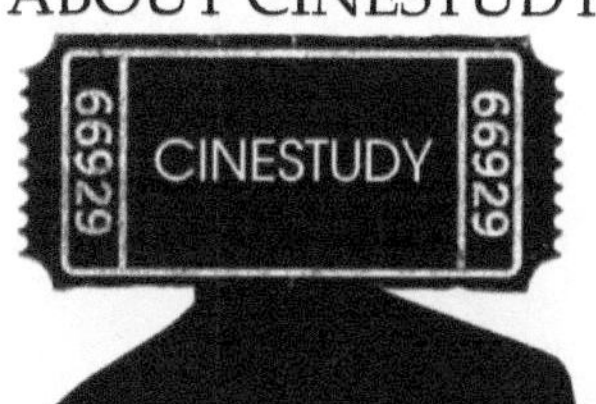 nominated instructional and interactive videos on the regional PBS series Framelines. The goal of Cinestudy is to allow anyone of any economic status to learn and practice the art of filmmaking.

www.cinestudyproject.org

www.ingramcontent.com/pod-product-compliance
Lightning Source LLC
Chambersburg PA
CBHW020920160726
47993CB00005B/2052